Changing Nebraska

By Thomas R. Walsh

Illustrated by
Sandy A. Peters

Edited by Betty Loudon

Published by the
Instructional Materials Council

Second Edition 1989

PREFACE

I wish to express sincere thanks to the Instructional Materials Council for making this work possible. The constant encouragement and support that I received from the executive committee and the president of the Council were sources of strength. The teacher review committee appointed by the executive committee took much time and offered many fine suggestions. To the membership of the teacher review committee I can only say thank you. I especially want to thank Dorothy Chapman. Without her continuous efforts this book would never have been written. Writing is one act, but the job of editing often goes unrecognized. In particular, I express my gratitude to Betty Loudon, staff member of the Nebraska State Historical Society. Kathy Sheahan was of great assistance in reviewing final copy and making editing suggestions.

The one person who is most deserving of my expression of appreciation is my wife, Edythe. She never complained about the weekend time I needed to finish the book. She only offered words of encouragement and her loving support.

Thomas R. Walsh

Lincoln, Nebraska
March 31, 1986

Acknowledgments

Special thanks to the members of the Advisory Committee for working with the author, Dr. Thomas Walsh.

Leola Bullock
Lincoln, Nebraska

Neal Cross
Lincoln, Nebraska

Alice Hayes
Imperial, Nebraska

Jordan Kominsky
Lincoln, Nebraska

Jeanne Lorenzen
Lincoln, Nebraska

Kathryn Martin
Grand Island, Nebraska

Margaret Rasmussen
Dorchester, Nebraska

Cindy Swanhorst
Lexington, Nebraska

Eugene Schneberger
Grand Island, Nebraska

Elizabeth Zimmerman
Lexington, Nebraska

Instructional Materials Council Executive Committee

Donald Vanderheiden
President

Glen Beran
Director

Dorothy Chapman
Executive Secretary

Gary Schmidt
Vice President

Eugene Schneberger
Director

Larry Harnish
Director

Members of a Lincoln multi-cultural awareness committee provided valuable assistance in reviewing the completed manuscript.

Table of Contents

S.A. PETERS

INTRODUCTION

Welcome to the story of Nebraska. Do you remember when you were a small child? If you were like me, you loved to hear stories. I used to sit upon the lap of my grandfather or grandmother, and they would tell wonderful stories. By the time I reached upper elementary school I found that I liked to write stories. It was fun for me to use my imagination and to create new settings and characters. I've never lost my interest in stories.

One day I decided to write a new story. It is the story I am about to share with you. The story of Nebraska is a true story. It took me a long time to write this story. I had to spend many hours finding information about Nebraska and its people. Writing the story of Nebraska was hard work, but it was also enjoyable.

Now that my story is finished, I have decided to dedicate it to you, the boys and girls of Nebraska. When a writer dedicates a piece of work, it means that the writer wants to give honor to a friend or to a special person. Please accept the honor I offer you. I do this because I have worked with boys and girls all my adult life as a teacher/educator. So to you, the youth of Nebraska, here is my story about the place where you live and the people who live there. I hope you enjoy the story and will take lots of time to think about it and to talk about it. One last thing—I would love to hear from you. Your teacher will know how to send letters to me. If there is something in the story that you find especially interesting, or if you want to tell me how parts of the story made you feel, please write to me. After all, the story of Nebraska is really a story about us, you and me. Isn't it? Think about it.

Your friend,
Dr. Tom Walsh

CHAPTER ONE
CHANGING NEBRASKA

Change Marches On

The story of Nebraska is a story about change. Change is a process which goes on all the time. It never stops. Sometimes change happens so gradually it is hard for us to notice. For example, when you look in the mirror, can you see differences in the way you look from day to day? Probably not. Your body changes slowly, and you do not feel yourself change.

Just for fun, find some photographs of yourself and your family taken when you were younger. See how much you have changed in a few short years! Have other members of your family changed?

The kinds of changes you see in yourself over a period of time happen to all things in the world. Nothing ever stays the same! Look at the photographs on the next page. See how Nebraska's largest city, Omaha, changed over its first one hundred years. What changes can you see that took place in Omaha? Why did those changes take place? Do you think Omaha is still changing? If so, how do you think Omaha is changing? How do you think your town is changing?

Photograph courtesy of the Nebraska State Historical Society

Omaha, Nebraska, 1850s

Photograph courtesy of the Nebraska State Historical Society

Omaha, Nebraska, 1950s

Layers of Change

Nebraska, like the city of Omaha, has experienced some big changes over time. It all started millions of years ago. So long ago that there were no human beings on earth. No one knows exactly what it was like in Nebraska then, or anywhere else on earth. There are scientists today who are called geologists (GE-OL-O-GISTS). They study the surface of the earth. Geologists (GE-OL-O-GISTS) have found that the earth is layered like an ice cream cone. Have you ever gone to an ice cream store and gotten a triple dip cone? Each dip is a layer of ice cream.

The same thing happened to the earth. In Nebraska, the layering was helped by the action of warm ocean water. Oceans in Nebraska! It is true, by studying the rocks and the earth's surface in Nebraska, geologists can find evidence that Nebraska was covered by water on different occasions. A great deal of material was deposited in Nebraska as a result of the gigantic forces in the earth which lifted up masses of rock far to the West and created the Rocky Mountains. The mountains were worn down by wind and water. Geologists know that rivers and wind carried soil and matter great distances from the Rockies and deposited them in Nebraska to help in the layering process. Finally, great sheets of ice called glaciers (GLA-CIERS) once covered Nebraska. When the glaciers (GLA-CIERS) melted they deposited huge amounts of rock, gravel, sand, and clay.

The Layering of Nebraska

If you had a gigantic x-ray machine which allowed you to take a picture of the state, you would see the layering of the earth. It might look like this:

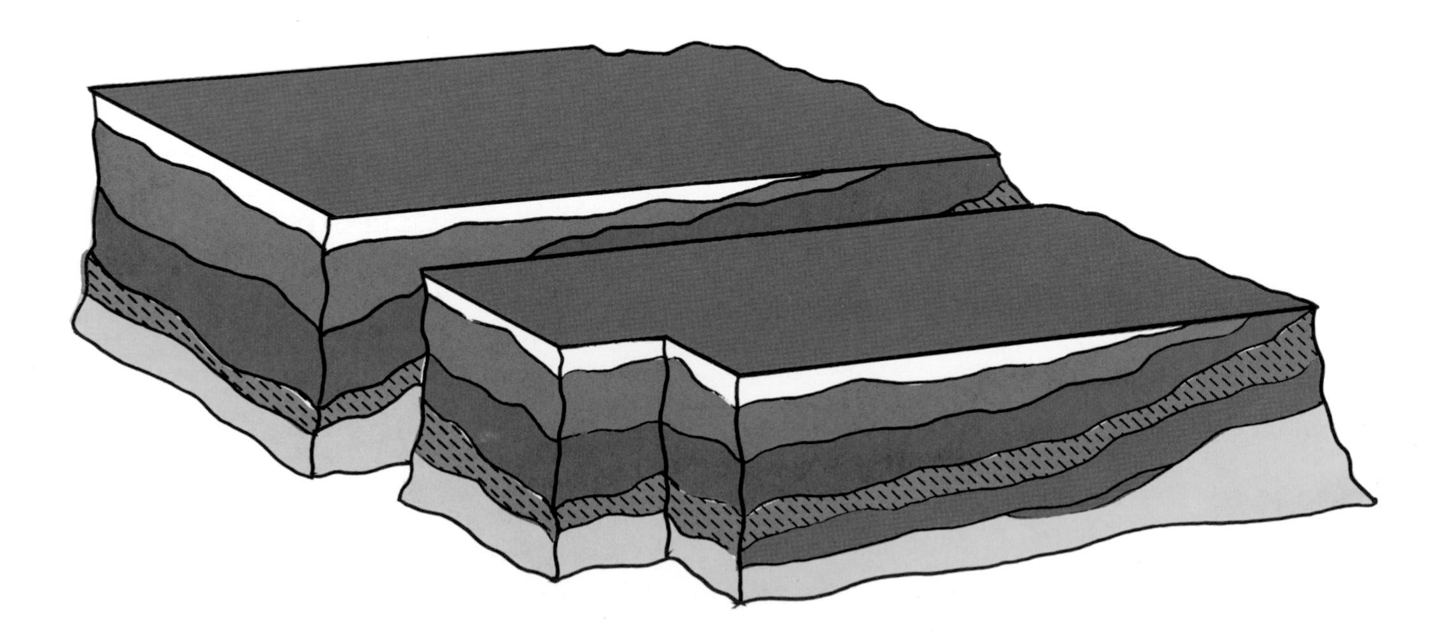

Nature Works Slowly

You know something about change. How long do you think it took for the different layers of the earth to be put in place by the forces of nature? If you guessed a few hundred or a few thousand years, you need to guess again. Geologists estimate that the world itself is over 5 billion years old. Look at that number—5,000,000,000.

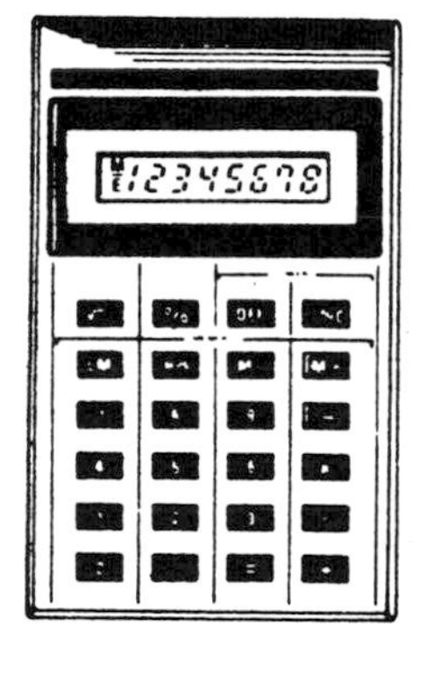

Subtract your birthdate from 5,000,000,000. That gives you a rough idea about how long ago nature started the job of putting the earth together. Try this—You are probably about ten years old. Divide 10 into 5,000,000,000. That will tell you about how many of your lifetimes ago the earth started forming. Hint—Use a calculator to divide 5,000,000,000 by your age.

Clues in the Rock

In Nebraska, geologists have looked for exposed rocks (rocks they can find on the surface). The oldest rocks they have been able to study are about 325 million years old. The very old bedrock is buried deep in the earth. As geologists study the rocks, they look for clues in the rocks to help them understand what Nebraska was like during these past 325 million years. The story of the earth is found in rocks because the rocks contain fossils (FOS-SILS). A fossil (FOS-SIL) is the hardened remains of a plant or of an animal that lived long ago. A fossil can also be only traces of a plant or an animal that lived long ago. For example, a geologist might find a large number of bones, teeth, shells, or scales in a layer of rock. This is all considered direct evidence of life that existed at one time. A geologist might also find footprints, leaves, burrows, or stems from plants in a layer of rock. This is considered indirect evidence of something that lived long ago.

A geologist is much like a detective. The job of a detective is to help solve a mystery. The detective must gather all the direct and indirect evidence found at the scene of a crime and piece together a story as to what may have happened and why. The same thing is true for a geologist. A geologist studies all the direct and indirect evidence found in the rocks of the earth and pieces together a story to tell what may have happened and why.

Clues in Nebraska Rock Explain the Past

By looking at the Time-Life Chart of Rocks Exposed in Nebraska, you begin to get some idea of how geologists have pieced the story of Nebraska together. Notice in the early years there were many life forms found in the seas that covered Nebraska. There were many small animals without backbones called invertebrates (IN-VER-TE-BRATES). (Do you know what you would call animals with backbones?) Eventually, fish and even sharks became common life forms in Nebraska.

Slowly, forces within the earth caused a great uplifting. This caused the seas covering Nebraska to drain away. As the seas drained away from the land, new life forms appeared. Fern trees which grow in warm climates dotted the land. Evidence of this tells geologists that Nebraska's climate was more moderate and warmer than it is today. There were reptiles (great lizards) who lived on the land. Over time, the world's greatest lizards made their appearance in Nebraska. Dinosaurs (DI-NO-SAURS), who lived both on land and in the sea, came on the scene. The seas eventually returned to Nebraska after another great uplifting elsewhere in the earth. The Rocky Mountains to the west towered high into the sky, twice as high as we know them today. As the seas started to drain again, the forces of water and wind carved at the Rockies and brought much rock, sand, gravel, and clay to Nebraska.

Pleistocene
Pliocene
Miocene
Oligocene
Cretaceous
CENOZOIC
MESOZOIC
PALEOZOIC
Permian
TIME-LIFE
CHART OF
ROCKS EXPOSED
IN NEBRASKA
Pennsylvanian

During this period new life came to Nebraska. Tigers, elephants, camels, and small horses made Nebraska their home. The climate was mild and much plant life grew. Then, about 20 million years ago, the area experienced another great uplifting. The Rocky Mountains, as we know them today, were created.

Other changes slowly began to happen. Temperatures started to fall about 2 million years ago. A huge sheet of ice, called a glacier (GLA-CIER), began forming in Canada and gradually moved southward. Glaciers (GLA-CIERS) moved into the United States on four different occasions. The first glacier, the Nebraskan, covered the eastern one-fourth of the state with ice several hundred feet thick and remained for about 100,000 years. The second glacier, the Kansan, covered eastern Nebraska for another one thousand centuries. Then came the Illinoian which stopped near Nebraska's northeast border. The last glacier, the Wisconsin, did not enter Nebraska. It began about 20,000 years ago and remained for about 2,000 years. The glaciers shaped some of the physical features of Nebraska by carving valleys and forming hills and plains. They also brought sand, rock, and clay which makes up much of Nebraska's surface and soil.

Important Ideas to Remember From Nebraska's Early Story

Change is something that happens all the time to everything on earth.

Great changes have taken place in Nebraska over millions of years. The land has changed. The climate has changed. Life forms have changed.

All of these changes took place before human beings entered Nebraska.

Things to Do

1. There are some special words used in telling the story about early Nebraska.

   GEOLOGY—GEOLOGIST
   FOSSIL
   DINOSAUR
   INVERTEBRATE
   GLACIER

   These are words one could use as guide words for going through the library card catalogue. If you are interested, you could find books to read that will tell you more about the earth and its early history. You can also use the guide words in finding information in encyclopedias.

2. Create your own story about early Nebraska. Use your imagination. With the information you have from this first chapter, you could probably write a story with a setting, characters, and a plot.
3. Use your imagination and draw a scene from Nebraska's early history. Think about a familiar place like your neighborhood or the place where your school is located. What would that place have looked like a million years ago, or any time in the distant past? What kind of life forms existed on or about that place?

CHAPTER TWO

PEOPLE COME

Digging For Clues

In the first part of Nebraska's story, you read about many changes that happened over millions of years. There were no human beings around to see those changes. As a matter of fact, human beings are newcomers to the Nebraska scene. How do you think the first human beings got to Nebraska? Where did they come from, and how long ago did they arrive in Nebraska? For the answers to those questions we have to rely upon a group of scientists called archaeologists (AR-CHAE-OL-O-GISTS). These are scientists who study about people who lived before people kept written records. An archaeologist (AR-CHAE-OL-O-GIST) digs into the earth and finds evidence of past life. Such things as pottery, tools, arrowheads, and spear points are the kinds of things an archaeologist looks for in the earth. Archaeologists also look for places where ancient (of times long ago) people may have had villages. By carefully digging into the earth and finding clues, archaeologists can piece together the story of past human life.

Through the work of archaeologists we know a great deal about how ancient people lived. We know the kinds of food ancient people ate. We know that some ancient people lived in villages. We know something about the dwellings used by ancient people. We even know about how long ago ancient people lived in Nebraska.

Photograph courtesy of the Nebraska State Historical Society

Archaeological Dig Site

Bands of Hunters Seek Food

If archaeologists can help put together the story of how ancient people lived, we still need to solve the riddle of how people got to Nebraska. If you study the map on this page, you will see the continents of Asia and North America. Notice where Nebraska is located on the North American continent. Follow the arrows that lead from Asia across the ocean area marked the Bering Strait. The arrows can be followed on to the North American continent, across Alaska and Canada, and down into the United States. There is reason to believe that at one time Asia and North America were joined together at the Bering Strait. This was probably like a land bridge that people and animals could walk across.

Scientists have found evidence that human beings have lived on the Asian continent for many thousands of years. These ancient people were hunters and gatherers. That is, they hunted animals for meat and they gathered fruit, bulbs, nuts, and plants to eat. Usually these ancient people lived in small groups called bands. Bands of hunters would range far and wide seeking food. Scientists think that about 40,000 years ago, or more, some bands of ancient people crossed over the land bridge at the Bering Strait and entered North America. This movement of people from Asia to North America went on for a long time. Like the changes that took place in early Nebraska, this new change of people coming into North America was slow but steady.

Gradually bands of hunters made their way towards what is now the central and south central United States. Little is known about these early hunters. They traveled on foot and hunted big animals like the mammoth (MAM-MOTH), a huge elephant that died out about 10,000 years ago. The ancient hunters used spears for weapons to kill the animals they hunted. Archaeologists have found stone spear points made by the early hunters. Spear points found in Nebraska show that the early hunters were here as long ago as 11,000 years.

Photograph courtesy of the Nebraska Games and Parks Commission with permission from Nebraska Historical Society

Clovis and Folsom Points

New Animals and New Challenges

As it always has been, things began to change. The glaciers melted and left the Nebraska area. The climate got warmer and drier. Lush grass began to grow across the prairies. The mammoth (MAM-MOTH) and other large animals died out, but they were replaced by bison (buffalo) who found the grass to be a rich source of food. Soon millions of buffalo lived in the area, and the hunters had a new source of food.

Life for the early hunters was difficult. Think what it would be like to face the storms of Nebraska without a permanent shelter. Sometimes the prairie grass would catch fire and a group of hunters, with no place to go for protection, could easily be burned in the fire. Buffalo herds could cover great distances in a single day, and it was impossible for the hunters to keep up with the herds. The early hunters had to be clever in order to survive.

Here is a challenge for you. Carefully study the picture on this page. Does the picture give you any clues about how the early hunters could have been successful in hunting animals?

Climate Change Affects People

The early hunters stayed in Nebraska until about 5000 B.C. (B.C. means before the birth of Christ; 5000 B.C. means five thousand years before the birth of Christ.) Then another change took place. A very serious drought set in and destroyed much plant life. The buffalo left and the hunters followed them into the woodland areas to the east and north.

Once again Nebraska experienced changes brought by the forces of nature. Archaeologists find little record of human life in Nebraska until about 2500 B.C. As the climate changed, other hunters came to Nebraska from the east. They lived a lifestyle similar to the earlier hunters. They used spears as their weapons and they gathered seeds, fruits, and plants. They hunted smaller animals since there was not an abundance of animals available.

In the early centuries of the Christian era (after the birth of Christ) a most important change took place in Nebraska. New people, called Woodland people, made their homes in the area. One thing archaeologists have discovered is that the Woodland people made pottery.

Before you go on in the reading, stop, think, and take a guess. Imagine that you are an archaeologist studying about past human life in Nebraska. As we have said in the reading, you have found spear points and animal bones that suggest to you the earliest people were hunters. One day you are examining an area you know was once occupied by Woodland people. You find pottery pieces and you manage to put together some rough pottery like you see in the drawing. You also find evidence that the Woodland people ate beans and squash. What conclusions can you draw? In what important ways are the Woodland people different from the early hunters? List your ideas on a piece of paper.

The First Farmers

Let's compare your ideas to that of archaeologists. You know that the earlier hunters had to be constantly seeking food. This meant that early hunters were always on the move. Their time was spent finding food for their existence. The Woodland people, since they made pottery, stayed in one place for a longer period of time (making pottery takes time). Although they hunted and gathered, they also planted crops. Some remains of food found by archaeologists show that the Woodland people grew beans and squash. To plant and to harvest gardens suggest that the Woodland people had to stay in one spot for longer periods of time. The Woodland people probably brought the seeds for such crops from the east and began growing crops in Nebraska. For the first time, human beings were using the soil of Nebraska as a resource to grow food.

The Village Dwellers

One idea about human history to remember is that change builds on change. In early Nebraska the changes came more slowly, but they were important. After people started using the land to grow crops, the climate continued to improve. More people came to Nebraska and a new seed was introduced. Maize (corn) became a highly important source of food. The bow and arrow were also introduced. Hunters could now use a lighter but more powerful weapon in killing game. These changes helped to establish a new way of life in Nebraska, the village life.

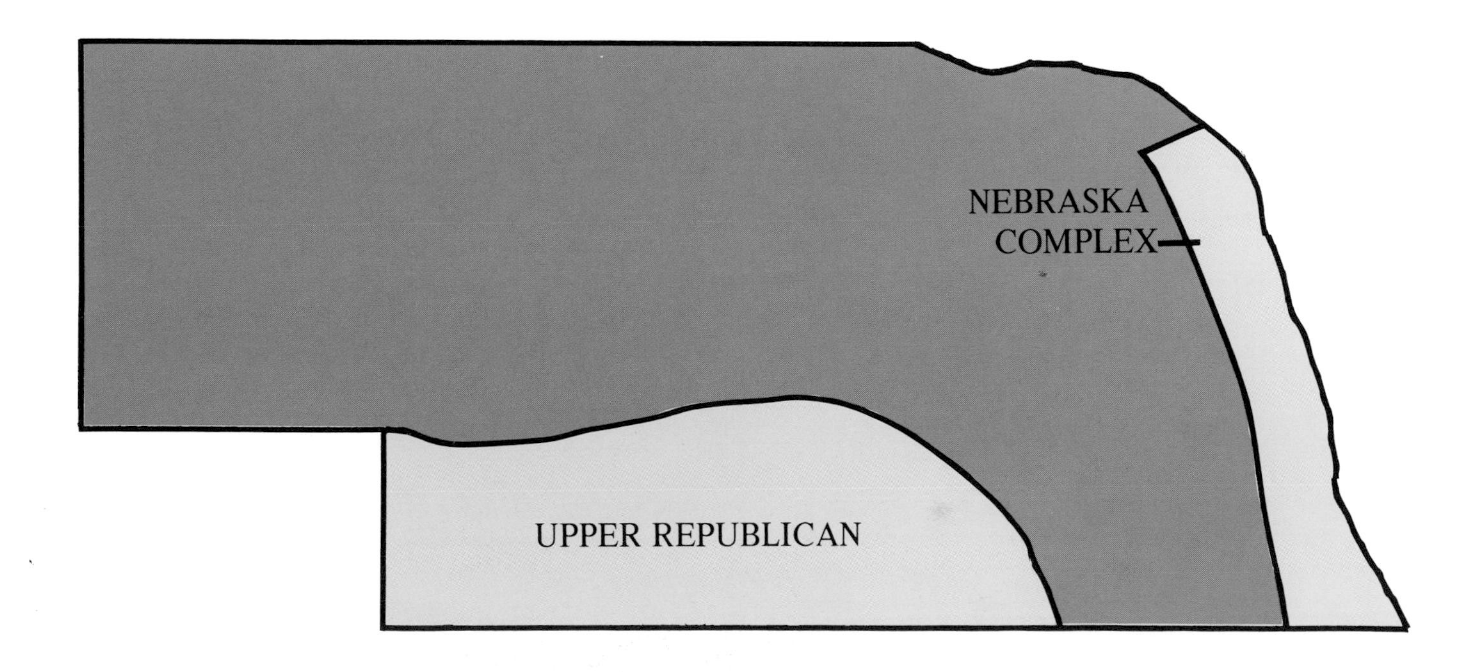

Starting about the year 900, village life in Nebraska grew more successful. The village dwellers built square-shaped earth lodges. The lodges were built near rivers and streams. The rich land along the waterways was good for growing crops. Anywhere from 50 to 100 people lived in the village sites, located in two major places in Nebraska. One group of villages stretched along the Missouri River. The other group of villages was located in a wide area along and between the Republican and Loup Rivers.

The village dwellers hunted buffalo as a major source of meat. They grew beans, corn, and squash on the land they cultivated (CUL-TI-VAT-ED). They made hoes from the shoulder blades of buffalo to work the land. The people who lived along the Missouri River were excellent at catching fish. Population in the villages grew as the people enjoyed a mixed way of life, depending upon both hunting and farming.

Sometime after the year 1300, the climate in Nebraska began to change once again. Another long drought settled on the area. The buffalo herds left to find new grasslands. The villagers could no longer grow enough crops to feed themselves. So after 400 years of good living, the village people of Nebraska gave up their villages and moved to other places.

Important Ideas to Remember About the Early People

The first people to come to Nebraska were hunters who traveled on foot and killed large animals using spears.

Nebraska's climate changes had great effects on the early people.

The mild climate attracted animals and early people to Nebraska.

The harsh climate caused animals and early people to leave Nebraska.

The Woodland people came from the east to become Nebraska's first farmers in the early centuries of the Christian era.

The village dwellers were successful in Nebraska as farmers and hunters for over 400 years.

Things to Do

1. There are some special words in this chapter about the early people of Nebraska.

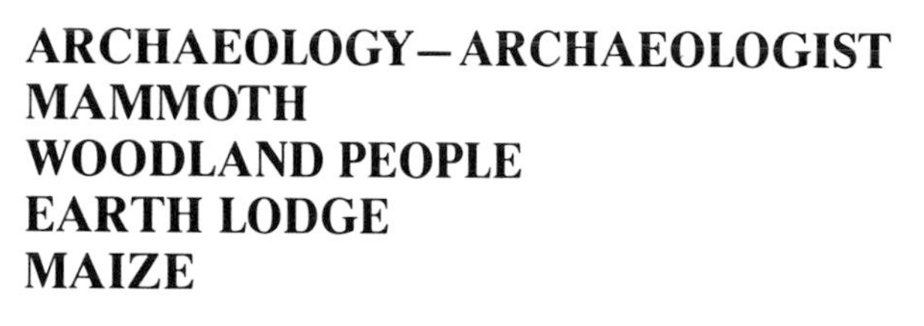

ARCHAEOLOGY—ARCHAEOLOGIST
MAMMOTH
WOODLAND PEOPLE
EARTH LODGE
MAIZE

   Use these words as guide words to find books and articles for reading about early people in North America and especially in Nebraska.

2. The Nebraska State Historical Society in Lincoln is responsible for finding out information about the history of Nebraska. The Historical Society employs archaeologists. If you are interested in Nebraska archaeology, write to the Historical Society. Ask for information about places in Nebraska where archaeologists have dug into the earth to make discoveries about early people.

CHAPTER THREE
NEW ARRIVALS

Keep Change in Mind

Nebraskans have an old saying they have repeated for many years. "If you don't like the weather, wait a minute." That saying is really a bit of "folk wisdom"—it comes from the people. It is funny, but is also true to some extent. The weather in Nebraska is changeable, and it does seem that sometimes Nebraska's weather can change in a minute. Do you recall a day when the weather seemed ideal? Maybe the sun was shining brightly without a cloud in the sky. Suddenly, dark clouds filled the sky, the wind picked up, the temperature dropped, and there you were in the middle of a thunderstorm. Has that ever happened to you?

Keep in mind Nebraska's changeable weather as you continue to read Nebraska's story. You already know that many changes took place in Nebraska during its early history. Geologists and archaeologists use the clues they find in Nebraska's rocks and soil to tell us much about early Nebraska. Sometime after the year 1500, many different people began to come to Nebraska. Like Nebraska's changeable weather, the coming of different people made for constant changes.

Each new group that came to Nebraska brought new ideas, different beliefs, a variety of goods and possessions, and new ways of life. As these different people met one another in Nebraska, they sometimes exchanged ideas, goods, and beliefs. When this happened, people's lives were changed. Such changes often took place suddenly. Sometimes when new people met one another in Nebraska, they did not get along. When this happened it often led to fighting, as one group of people tried to control another group of people. The result of violent fighting was always more change in how people lived.

One thing you should always remember: we cannot change what has happened between people in the past, be it good or bad. If we learn about what happened to people in the past, however, we can discover ways that will help all people get along better today and in the future.

Old and New

When people returned to Nebraska following the great drought, two different ways of life took shape. The two ways of life had been known in Nebraska before, and they soon took root once again.

Village Life

Village people were like the early village dwellers. They lived in villages usually located along important waterways. The village people generally came to Nebraska from the south and east. They were hunters and farmers, and they became well established in eastern and central Nebraska.

Nomadic Life

Nomadic (NO-MAD-IC) people were like the early hunters in Nebraska. They were people who did not have a fixed or permanent home. These people generally came to Nebraska from the north, the east, and the west. They lived by hunting and gathering. Nomadic (NO-MAD-IC) people followed the buffalo herds. They hunted the buffalo as a source of meat and raw material. The nomadic way of life became well established in western Nebraska.

Tribal Life

Both the village and the nomadic people belonged to groups called tribes. A tribe is a group of people who live together. Usually a tribe is made up of many different families. Members of a tribe will speak a common language and share important beliefs. Individual members within a tribe are often responsible for certain work. Since people and families live so closely together within a tribal group, they develop a great respect and concern for each other. Tribal members are loyal to their own tribe. It is through one's tribe that a person has a sense of belonging and acceptance.

Think about this. If you live in a town that has a basketball or football team and have attended games, you probably feel a sense of loyalty towards your team. Have you, along with other people supporting your team, sung the team song or cheered together for the team?

Do you belong to a religious group? If so, do the people in your group worship together? Do the members of your group try to help one another? If a member of your group is sick or in need, do the other members try to help the person or family in need? Do you feel proud being a member of your group?

This may give you some idea of how people who belong to a tribe feel about each other and about their tribe. Tribal members are proud people who always have a home within their tribe. Being a member of a tribe is a great gift.

Two Ways of Life

The tribal groups that came to Nebraska were different from one another. Each group had its own language and beliefs, but tribal groups did exchange ideas and goods. In this way all tribal groups came to accept either the village way of life or the nomadic way of life. Two of the earliest tribes we know about in Nebraska were the Pawnee and the Apache Indians. The Pawnee were village dwellers and at one time were the largest tribal group in Nebraska. The Apache were nomadic hunters who roamed over large areas of western Nebraska.

Village Tribal Life

The largest village tribal group in Nebraska was the Pawnee. Archaeologoists believe the Pawnee originally came to Nebraska from the southwestern and southeastern United States. Some scientists think the earlier village dwellers in Nebraska were related to the Pawnee. The Pawnee had tribal relatives who lived in other nearby states.

When they first arrived in Nebraska, the Pawnee built large villages along the big rivers. As their population grew, they built smaller villages along streams. Their villages spread out from the Missouri, Republican, Platte, and Loup River systems (see map).

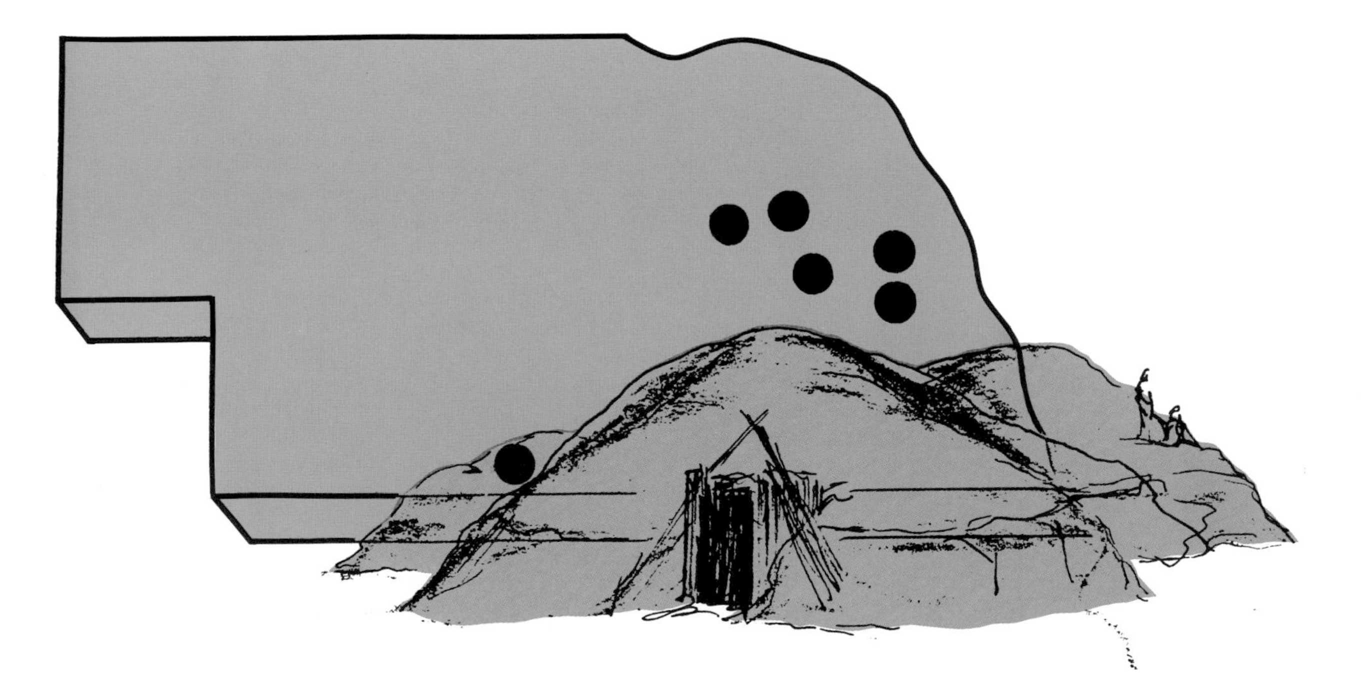

Historic Pawnee Sites

The Pawnee built large, round earth lodges. The Pawnee lodges were well suited to Nebraska's climate. They were reasonably warm in the winter and cool in the summer. The Pawnee made their lodges by putting up strong wooden frames and rafters. Then they covered the wooden frames and rafters with brush and dirt. The Pawnee lodges were large enough to house up to forty people. Depending on the size of the village, there might be anywhere from 4 to 15 lodges in the village.

Photograph courtesy of the Nebraska State Historical Society

Pawnee Earth Lodge

After 10 to 15 years, the lodge framing would rot and the lodge would fall in. Before this happened, villagers would move to a new site and construct new lodges. They did this because they had probably used most of the available timber in the old village site for building lodges and for firewood. It was easier to move to a new site than to haul heavy timber to an old site.

The Pawnee people were excellent farmers. Remember, they had no powerful tools or horses, so they had to use hoes to break the ground. The prairie grasslands were much too tough for them to break, so they used the land near rivers and streams for garden plots. They planted squash, beans, and sunflowers. Corn, however, was their main crop. They waited for the right signs from nature before they planted. After the plants had sprouted, they hoed twice to keep the weeds down and allow the plants to grow stronger. After the second hoeing of corn, it was time for the summer buffalo hunt.

Nearly all the people in the village joined in the hunt. Only the very old, handicapped, or sick were allowed to stay behind. The people packed up what they needed and walked several days to buffalo country. Here they broke into small hunting bands. Like the hunters of old, the Pawnee waited at watering holes and other likely places to kill the buffalo. Sometimes hunters waited near a cliff. When the buffalo came to the area to graze, they would chase the buffalo toward the edge and drive them over the cliff. The buffalo were either killed or injured in the fall. Then the hunters cut away the meat. Much of the meat was cut into strips and dried for future eating. The hides were removed and used for making leather. From the hides the Pawnee made tipi covers, clothing, and bags.

After a period of hunting, perhaps a month or more, the people would return to their villages with great supplies of meat and hides. Dogs were often used to pull travoises (TRA-VOISES). A travois (TRA-VOIS) was a device used to haul things. It was made from two poles tied together with leather (see drawing).

Once back in the village, the people worked the skins from the hunt. That is, they made the skins ready to be used in making things. In August the villagers picked the early corn. The corn was roasted in the husk. After roasting, the grains were removed and dried in the sun for storage. This was to be food for winter use. Other corn was allowed to fully ripen in September. The September corn was then dried in the sun, shelled, and put into storage pits. The best ears were set aside to be used as seed corn the next year.

Following the corn harvest, it was time for the fall buffalo hunt. October was a good time for hunting buffalo. The animals had grown a full coat of hair by October. The hides were excellent for making warm winter robes. Also, the meat was at its best. The buffalo had fed on the rich grass all summer putting on weight for the winter.

The fall hunt was usually made up of several small hunts. In this manner, the Pawnee feasted on fresh meat for some time while working the hides into winter robes. In addition to buffalo, the Pawnee also hunted antelope, deer, elk, and other smaller animals.

Other village tribes who settled in eastern Nebraska followed a pattern of life much like the Pawnee. Five important tribal groups—the Oto, the Omaha, the Ponca, the Iowa, and the Missouria—came later. They learned to build earth lodges. They also grew corn and hunted buffalo in summer and fall.

Nomadic Tribal Life

The Apache tribal group came to Nebraska from the north. The Apache people migrated (moved) from Canada in a southerly direction over a long period of time. Some of the Apache people traveled into Texas. Many Apache bands spread out across a large area which includes parts of Nebraska and other nearby states.

Since the Apache were nomads, it is more difficult for archaeologists to find clues about how they lived. We know they traveled on foot. The Apache had well-trained dogs. These animals were used as pack animals. The dogs carried things or pulled travoises which were loaded with goods. Traveling around as they did, the Apache people owned few large or heavy possessions. They lived in tents. You could call their tents the earliest style tipis. The tents were made of wooden poles and covered with animal skins

Apache Tent

that were sewn tightly together. The tents of the Apache could be transported easily and had the advantage of being easy to set up and take down. Like the earth lodges of the Pawnee, the Apache tents were warm in the winter and cool in the summer.

The Apache were excellent hunters. In fact, they were such good hunters they began trading meat and hides for corn, squash, and beans. They often traded with village tribal groups who lived west of Nebraska.

Other nomadic tribes came to this area at a later time. One important group was the Dakota people. The Dakota were divided into three main bodies: the Western, the Middle, and the Eastern. The Western Dakota were nomadic and had great influence on the history of Nebraska and the United States. The Middle Dakota were also nomadic. They occupied territory north of Nebraska, and they had great influence on the history of Nebraska. Other nomadic people who played an important part in the state's history were the Cheyenne, the Arapaho, and the Commanche tribes. Members of these tribes were great buffalo hunters.

More to Come

Can you tell that life in Nebraska was starting to change? People were coming to Nebraska in greater numbers. They hunted, farmed, and even began trading with other people in nearby areas. The stage was set for greater changes as you will learn in the coming chapters. What do you think happened that was to cause great changes for the nomadic and village people of Nebraska?

Important Ideas to Remember About the New Arrivals

Following the great drought, people in Nebraska established two important ways of life.

1. Village life was found in eastern and central Nebraska. People lived in earth lodges along rivers and streams. These people were farmers and hunters.
2. Nomadic life was found in western Nebraska. People lived in tents, traveled on foot, and hunted buffalo. These people were hunters and traders.

Both village people and nomadic people lived in tribal groups.
The Pawnee were the largest single tribal group in Nebraska at one time.
The Pawnee were village dwellers. They were excellent farmers and hunters.
The Apache were the earliest nomadic tribal group in Nebraska.
The Apache were excellent hunters.

Things to Do

1. Guaranteed interesting reading can be found by using the following guide words. Search the card catalogue and use the encyclopedias. Don't pass up this opportunity.

   NOMAD – NOMADIC
   PAWNEE TRIBE or PAWNEE INDIANS
   APACHE TRIBE or APACHE INDIANS
   TRAVOIS
   EARTH LODGE

2. Paint pictures with words. Have you written poetry before? This chapter is full of ideas for making beautiful statements. Let me share two statements with you that I wrote after thinking about the early Pawnee and Apache of Nebraska. You can create similar word paintings.

WITHIN ME – A NEBRASKAN
by Tom Walsh

Earth lodge and hoe
No clock but the seasons
They planted and harvested
Mother Corn gave them plenty

The Hunt was their life
Nebraska their home.
In the past they are us
Forever we roam.

CHAPTER FOUR
EUROPEANS BRING CHANGE

Change—The Great Multiplier

What ideas did you have about the causes for great changes that affected the village people and the nomadic people of Nebraska many years ago? Do you remember these ideas from our story so far? Change happens all the time. One change builds on another change. When change builds upon change, it has a multiplying effect. Here is an example of the multiplying effect.

When the automobile was invented, people said it was a great invention. Now people could travel from one place to another faster. This was a wonderful change. Soon millions of people wanted automobiles. The one single change, the invention of the automobile, led to other changes. Roads had to be built for the automobile to travel upon. Much land was taken out of farm production to build roads. People had to pay money (taxes) to the government to build the roads and to keep them repaired. Automobiles needed fuel, so more oil had to be found and taken out of the ground to provide gasoline and oil to run the automobiles. Automobiles were involved in many accidents. More police had to be hired to keep the roads and streets safe. Laws had to be written that established driving rules. Of course, the fuel automobiles burn gives off poisonous gases. This has led to air pollution problems, especially in large cities where more automobiles are driven.

There were many more changes brought about by the invention of the automobile. You can begin to understand how one important change leads to other changes. This is a multiplying effect. A diagram that shows a few of the changes brought about by the invention of the automobile might look like this:

INVENTION OF THE AUTOMOBILE

MORE ROADS
MORE LAWS
MORE LAND TAKEN FOR ROADS
MORE TAXES
MORE AIR POLLUTION
MORE OIL NEEDED

You might want to think about important changes that have happened in your life. Draw out a diagram for a few important changes. Show other changes that have come about because of a single important change. Remember, as more change takes place, the faster change happens.

The Coming of Europeans

Change happened very fast in Nebraska once Europeans came to the new world. Here is a change diagram that will help you identify some of the big changes that resulted from one important change, the coming of Europeans to the Americas.

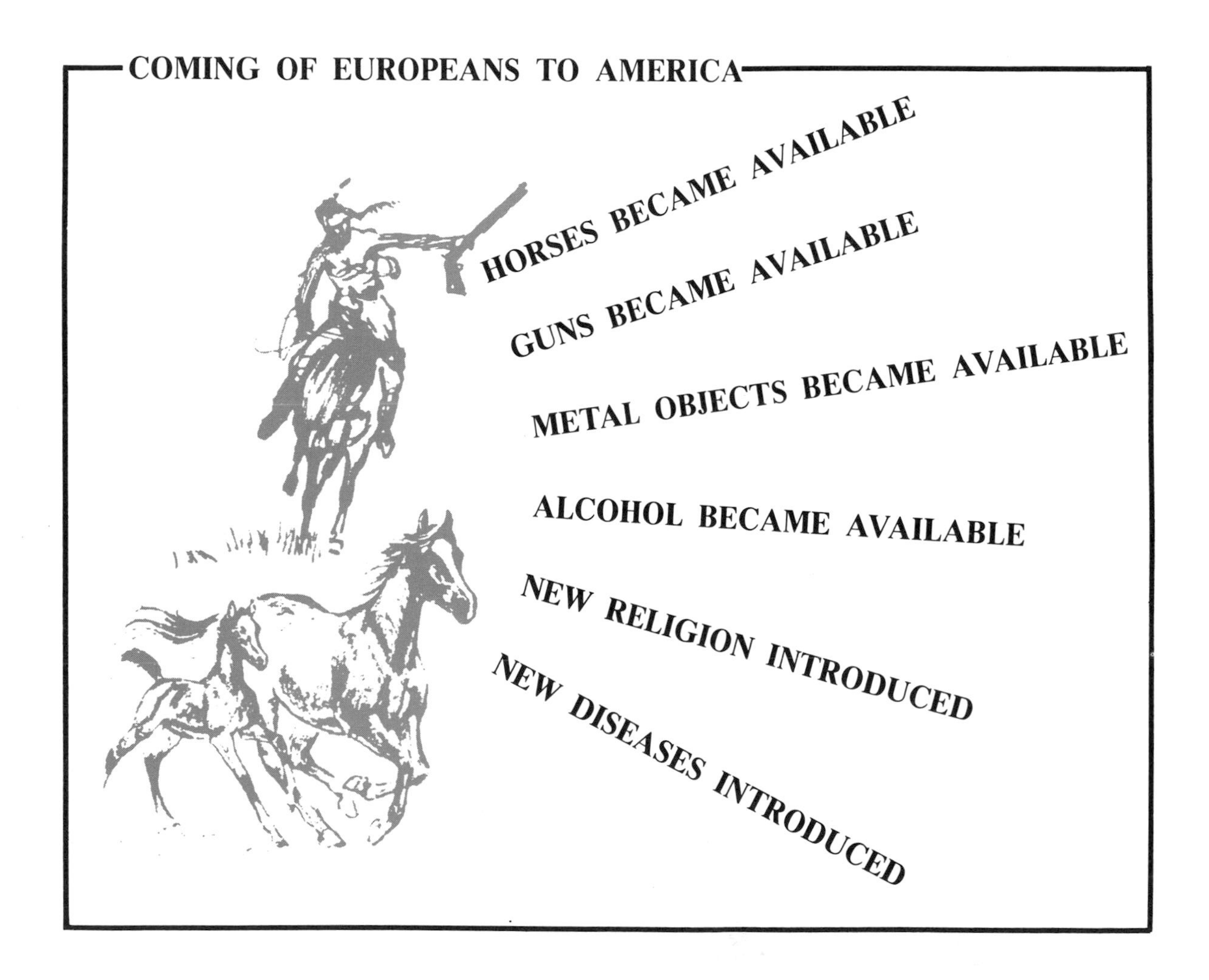

Before you read any further, think about the change diagram dealing with the coming of Europeans. From what you know about how the village and nomadic peoples lived in Nebraska, how would the coming of Europeans to the Americas change life in Nebraska?

OPERATION EUROPE—Who are the Europeans?
Your job—1. Find a globe of the world. Do you have a globe in your classroom? If not, where would you find one in your school? 2. Locate the continent of Europe on the globe. 3. Find these three countries. They are European countries that helped to bring great changes to Nebraska: England (United Kingdom), France, and Spain. 4. Locate the United States on the globe. 5. Find Nebraska's location in the United States. 6. Write a short answer to the question, "Who are the Europeans?"

Why Europeans Came

Hundreds of years ago, the countries of England, France, and Spain were great rivals. They were the world's most powerful nations. One reason they were so powerful is that they all had big navies. If you look at the globe again, you will find that each of these countries is located near the ocean. In 1492, three Spanish ships under Captain Christopher Columbus sailed from Spain to a small island in the Bahamas (BA-HA-MAS). Find the Bahamas (BA-HA-MAS) on the globe. Use your finger as a ship. Starting at Spain, move your finger to the Bahamas. Columbus did not know of North and South America. He thought he had sailed to Asia and thought he had arrived in a place called the East Indies. When he met dark-skinned people, he called them "Indians."

After Columbus reached America, other European countries became interested in America, especially England and France. Since England, France, and Spain were rivals, each country wanted to find riches and claim land for itself. Other European explorers came to the new world. The Europeans were interested in trading with the native people. They were also interested in bringing the Christian religion to the "Indians." Most Europeans, however, did not respect the beliefs of the native people. The Europeans took the land away from the native people. Land in the new world taken in the name of a European country was called a colony (COL-O-NY).

When you look at the map, you will see that Spain claimed all of Mexico and Florida as a colony by the year 1521. The Spanish made the Indian people their slaves. They forced the native people to work on big farms and to take care of their cattle and horses. The Spanish even sent an explorer

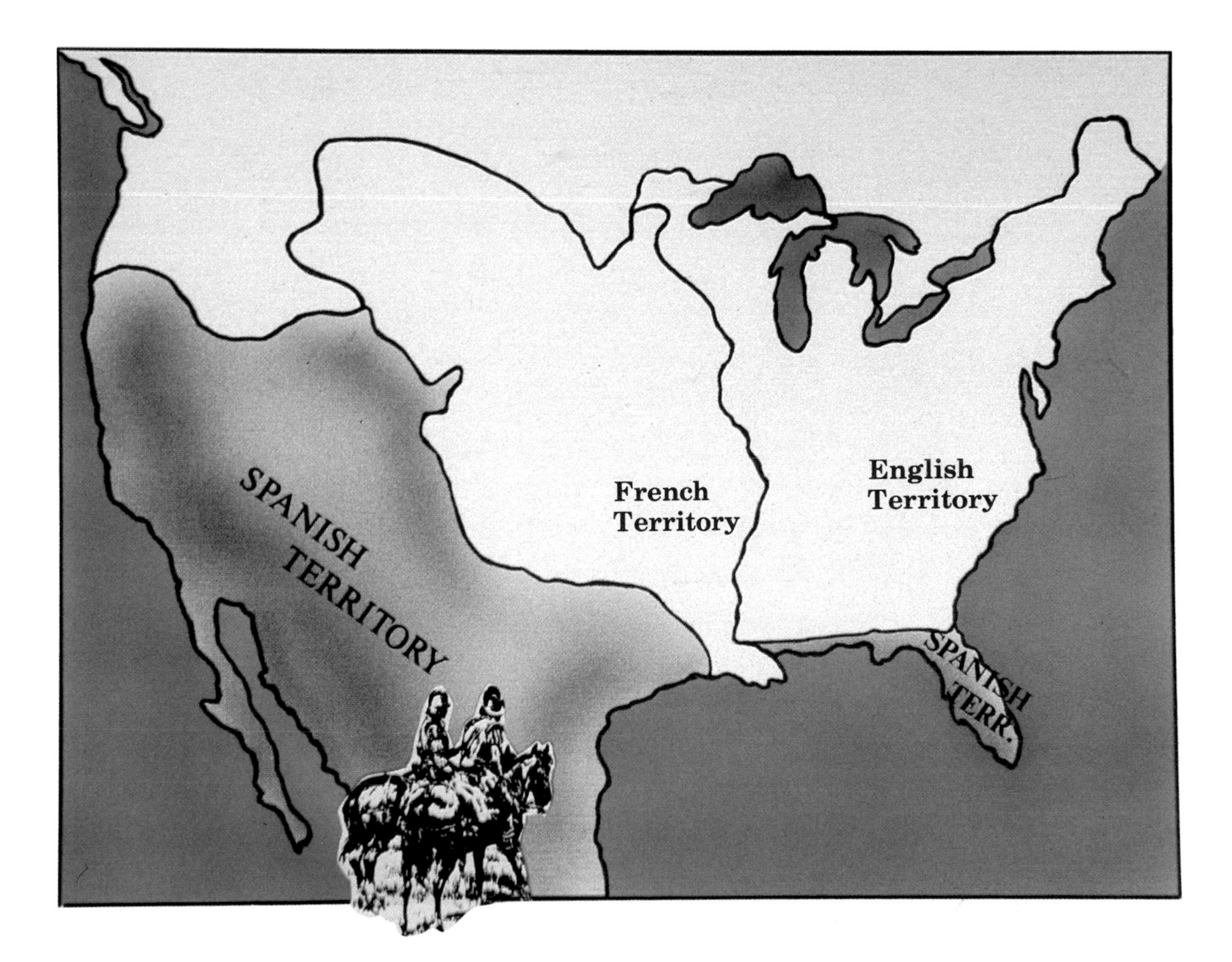

named Francisco Coronado (KOR-UH-NAH-DOH) into the area near Nebraska in 1541–42. Coronado thought he would find gold. Instead he found tribal village people living in earth lodges.

Over a period of years, England set up colonies (COL-O-NIES) on the Atlantic coast of America. The French set up colonies on the St. Lawrence River, explored the Mississippi River, and established the city of New Orleans. Spain moved into California, Arizona, New Mexico, and Texas (see map). The countries of Spain, France, and England wanted to become richer and more powerful through their colonies in America. They fought great battles against each other on the oceans and on land.

Europeans Affect Nebraskans

Although the people of Nebraska had little contact with Europeans at first, the Europeans had great influence on Nebraskans. The Spanish had brought horses to Mexico. Since the Spanish had made slaves of the Indian people, many tribal members from northern Mexico escaped slavery by taking Spanish horses. They rode the horses north and lived with members of the Apache tribe. In this manner the Apache were able to get horses. Once the Apache learned to handle horses, they raided the Spanish settlements and took more horses. Soon the Apache were horse rich. In their trading with other tribes, the Apache traded horses for goods they needed. By the year 1776, when the American Declaration of Independence was signed, native people from Mexico to Canada owned horses.

A SPECIAL AMERICAN HOLIDAY—Look at the map of the English Atlantic Coast colonies on page 33. On July 4, 1776, people living in these colonies said they were no longer English citizens. They "declared" themselves to be "independent"—Declaration of Independence. This means the people living in these colonies told the whole world they were going to rule themselves and not be ruled by England any longer. Later these colonies formed a union (group) called the United States of America. This was the beginning of our country. We celebrate our country's birthday each year on July 4th, a special holiday for all Americans.

The multiplier effect of owning horses was great. It was easier for the nomadic tribes to hunt buffalo. More people could be fed and the population of the nomadic tribes grew. The people had more hides for tipis, robes, and clothing. They no longer needed dogs. Remember, dogs ate meat. Dogs needed the same type of food used by the tribal members. Horses ate grass and grain. Horses could live off the rich grasslands, the same grassland the buffalo used for food. Horses allowed the native people to enjoy a better way of life.

The coming of the horse was not always helpful. Since native people could travel more freely on horseback, members of different tribal groups came into more frequent contact with one another. This often led to warfare. The Apache became fierce horseback warriors. Knowing the Spanish always needed slaves, the Apache started raiding the villages of the village people. They captured many Pawnee people and took them south to New Mexico where the Pawnee were sold into slavery. The village people had a difficult time trying to defend against the Apache horsemen.

A strange thing began to happen over a period of time. The Apache took many Pawnee women as captives. Some scientists think the Pawnee women taught the Apache how to build earth lodges and grow corn. Apache life began to change from nomadic life to village life. As the Apache began to live more like the Pawnee, Apache villages became targets for raids.

Changes caused by the coming of the Europeans were keenly felt in Nebraska by the early 1700's. The French traders had explored the Mississippi River and the Missouri River. They began trading with the Pawnee. The French were interested in furs, and in return they gave the Pawnee guns and other metal objects. The Pawnee used these weapons to fight the Apache. With this new power, the Pawnee were able to capture many Apache. The captured Apache were sold to the French as slaves to be taken back to St. Louis and New Orleans.

Not only did the Pawnee have guns, but the Commanche, a tribal group that lived in the Rocky Mountains, had acquired many horses. The Commanche became great horsemen. These excellent warriors started to raid the Apache villages where they took food, horses, and captives to be used as slaves. Finally, large numbers of Apache fled south to New Mexico where they asked the Spanish for help to protect them from the Commanche. About the time the Declaration of Independence was signed in 1776, some Apache fled to Arizona into the White Mountains. These proud people who had been great buffalo hunters in Nebraska, Colorado, and Kansas now took up a new life in the American Southwest, far from the buffalo on the plains.

Only the Beginning

Now you can begin to understand what started to happen in Nebraska. A special way of life developed for native people. Both the nomadic and village people obtained horses. They also obtained new weapons they could use in hunting and in warfare. We can call this new way of life the Horse and Buffalo Culture (CUL-TURE). When a group of people live together and behave in ways that are alike, scientists call this a culture (CUL-TURE). At this time, several tribal groups lived in Nebraska. They spoke different languages and they had different beliefs, but they all used horses and hunted buffalo. Warfare, like that which happened between the Apache, the Commanche, and the Pawnee, also became a part of the Horse and Buffalo Culture.

In the next chapter you will read more about the Horse and Buffalo Culture. For now, it is well to recall how different life was becoming for Nebraskans. Remember the early hunters and gatherers who used stone-tipped spears to hunt the big animals of long ago? Remember the early village dwellers and how they struggled to live by hunting and growing crops? The coming of the Europeans brought new promises and new problems for the people of Nebraska. What do you think were the promises and problems for the people of the Horse and Buffalo Culture?

Important Ideas to Remember About the Changes Brought by Europeans

Change builds upon change.
People don't always expect the many changes that can come from a single important change.
Europeans are people who live on or come from the continent of Europe.
The French, the Spanish, and the British (or English) are Europeans who came to America to acquire land and wealth.
The Europeans established colonies in America and were in competition with each other.
Europeans brought new goods and ideas to America.
European goods and ideas affected the native people in America.
Horses and guns were two European possessions that caused great changes for the people of Nebraska.

Things to Do

1. Guide words galore to be explored through this chapter. Latch on to the word trail and see where it leads you!

   EUROPE—EUROPEANS
   CHRISTOPHER COLUMBUS
   EXPLORER
   MEXICO
   AMERICAN COLONIES
   COMMANCHE TRIBE or COMMANCHE INDIANS
   GREAT PLAINS
   CULTURE

2. Something to talk about. Hold a class discussion about what happened to the Native Americans when they first met the Europeans. The Europeans thought Christianity was a religion the native people should accept. They took land from the native people. In some cases they forced native people into slavery. Why did that happen? Do people still act that way towards one another? Are there ways that you can think of which would help people live together in peace?

   There is a song that you have probably heard. This song has a verse which says: "Let there be peace on earth and let it begin with me." What does that verse mean?

CHAPTER FIVE

THE HORSE AND BUFFALO CULTURE

Servant and Friend

Mobility (MO-BIL-I-TY) is a word you may have heard before. It means one is able to move about freely. Americans have great mobility (MO-BIL-I-TY). People in America use automobiles, trucks, airplanes, trains, boats, and bicycles to get around. In the recent past, the horse was the most common vehicle. Although not as common today, there are still people in our state who use the horse as a vehicle. Some of you may ride a horse to school! Whether you have ever ridden a horse or not, the horse has played an important part in Nebraska's story.

Conduct a survey. Discover the importance of the horse in the recent past. Check with parents, grandparents, other relatives, teachers, and local senior citizens. How many have owned horses? How many have used horses for transportation? How many have used horses for work animals? How many have used horses for pleasure riding? If you find people who have owned or used horses, do they have any interesting stories about horses they would be willing to share with you? If you find people who have been around horses, did they discover something about themselves through horses?

Personal Note From The Author—My father grew up on a farm and used horses all his early life for transportation and as work animals. He always told me that he learned more about kindness from being around horses than from any other experience in life. Why do you think that happened?

Horses Change Nebraska

In Nebraska during the early 1800's, life began to center around the horse. More tribal groups came to Nebraska because the horse allowed people to travel greater distances to hunt buffalo. The Cheyenne, for example, were a tribal group that once lived near the Great Lakes (find the Great Lakes on a map). Many years ago they moved westward where they met the villagers living along the Missouri River. For a while the Cheyenne lived like the villagers by farming and building earth lodges. In the late 1700's, the Cheyenne people got horses and began to pursue the buffalo. They moved into what is now western Nebraska and South Dakota. They gave up farming and pottery making. They depended upon the buffalo for their basic needs, food and shelter. They used the buffalo to trade for other goods.

Even the Pawnee, the great village dwellers, were affected by the ownership of horses. The Pawnee became great horse handlers. The Pawnee people came to own so many horses that they lacked enough grass around their villages to feed the animals. The people began to spend more time on the hunt and less time in the villages. While on the hunt, the Pawnee lived in skin tipis just like the nomads. During the time on the hunt the earth lodges sat empty. Hunting became so important to the Pawnee that they no longer made some of the fine pottery their people had made in earlier days. Many of the crafts that were once important in village life were given up.

The Dakota were another important group of people who came to Nebraska to take up a new life. Remember our mention of the Dakota nation in Chapter Three? The tribal groups that made up the Dakota nation are often called the Sioux. They lived in the lake country of Minnesota (find Minnesota on a map). Some members of the Dakota nation lived by hunting while others farmed, gathered, and hunted. The Western, or Teton Dakota, were great hunters. Around 1750, the Teton obtained horses. They called the horses "sacred dogs" and believed horses were special gifts to be used by them. With horses, Western Dakota hunters traveled great distances in search of buffalo.

Within a short time, Dakota hunters entered South Dakota and Nebraska. The Western Dakota made friends with the Cheyenne and another tribal group called the Arapaho. Members of these three tribes hunted and lived in the Wyoming, South Dakota, and western Nebraska area for many years.

Other tribal groups belonging to the Dakota nation also moved across the Missouri River. Tribal groups of the Middle Dakota came to occupy what is now North and South Dakota. They, too, had great influence on Nebraska history.

Keep in mind that the native people in Nebraska lived as village dwellers and nomads. First they obtained horses, and later they obtained guns and other goods from the Europeans traders and others.

BRAIN TEASER—What does this statement mean?

The horse made native people more independent. Guns, knives, axes, cloth, and other goods obtained from the Europeans and the traders made the native people more dependent.

Here is a good plan.

1. Use the dictionary to look up the words independent and dependent.
2. Write down what you think the statement means.
3. Discuss what you think the statement means with your classmates.
4. Reach an agreement, as a class, about what the statement means.
5. As a class, decide why the statement is important.

Important Ideas to Remember About the Horse and Buffalo Culture

The horse gave greater mobility to the native people.

More tribal groups came to Nebraska because they had horses to use in hunting the buffalo.

The horse affected the village dwellers by making them more dependent upon the buffalo for food and materials.

The two ways of life, village and nomadic, continued to be important to the native people even after the arrival of the horse.

Things to Do

1. Hopefully, you have taken time as you have been studying about Nebraska to use the chapter guide words in finding books and articles. Here are some more guide words that can help you to discover GOLD!

   TRANSPORTATION
   CHEYENNE TRIBE or CHEYENNE INDIANS
   ARAPAHO TRIBE or ARAPAHO INDIANS
   DAKOTA INDIANS

2. The horse became the single most important cause for change for the native people in Nebraska. Do you think there is one single thing in your life today that will bring great change for you and others in the future? Think about it. Talk to your parents and to other members of your family. Bring your ideas to class and see how your ideas compare with those of your classmates.

CHAPTER SIX

LIFE IN THE HORSE AND BUFFALO CULTURE

Things Human Beings Share in Common

Human beings, wherever they live on earth and no matter what language they speak, share some things in common. All people need to eat. People generally wear some form of clothing to keep their bodies warm and to protect themselves. People usually have a set of beliefs that guide their lives. All people share music and art. People always have some form of government which sets rules and protects the group. People always have some type of family organization.

Stop and think about how those things apply to you. What are your favorite foods to eat? How about clothing? Do you have some favorite clothes you like to wear? Do you dress differently for different occasions? Do you wear more clothes in the winter than you do in the summer? Do you belong to a church or a religious group? If not, are there some beliefs that you and members of your family think are important? Do those beliefs in any way affect how you behave? Can you think of some rules set down by government which limit your behavior yet protect you? Do you like to listen to music? Do you like to sing at times? Have you ever drawn or seen a picture that means something special to you? Are you a member of a family? In being a member of a family, do you feel that you give and receive love? Do the members of your family help and support one another?

In many ways native people who lived during the time of the Horse and Buffalo Culture lived much like you, but there were differences. Young people did not go to school. They were taught by their parents, grandparents, relatives, and elders how to be good and successful members of their tribe. Your family probably buys much of your food and clothing. In the Horse and Buffalo Culture, family members were responsible for obtaining their food and materials to make clothing directly from the plants and animals found in their area. Just like you, native people who lived in the Horse and Buffalo Culture had fun games that they played. They laughed and they danced. They shared their successes and failures. But, as we have seen before, nothing ever stays the same. Change came very suddenly for the Horse and Buffalo people, and we can all learn from what happened.

Horse and Buffalo Culture Life

Beliefs

Of the highest importance to all native people were their beliefs. There were many different tribes in Nebraska and they held different beliefs. In general, the people of all tribes believed in the Great Mystery. The Great Mystery was found everywhere. Animals that were killed and used, plants that were used or eaten, all of the things of nature were gifts of the Great

Mystery. Native people took what was necessary to live from nature and were thankful to the Great Mystery.

It was common for native people to go alone to a special place, like on a hill, and ask the Great Mystery for mercy. Sometimes people would not eat or drink for several days before they prayed. They believed this would give them inner strength to walk the good path.

The beliefs of the native people affected everything they did. When European and other settlers came to Nebraska, they would not accept the beliefs of the native people. Some white people wanted the native people to become Christians. The native people usually accepted some Christian beliefs, but whites seldom respected the beliefs of the native people. This led to much trouble between the whites and native people.

Action and Beliefs

Have you ever heard the saying "nobody's perfect"? When a person makes a mistake, you might hear that person excuse his or her mistake by saying "nobody's perfect." All human beings make mistakes. Maybe you have put something together wrong. Maybe you have made a mistake in your math while trying to solve a problem. We have all made those kinds of mistakes.

There is another kind of mistake which we feel inside. Do you believe you should be kind to other people? Have you ever been mean to somebody? If you have, you probably knew that was wrong. It was a mistake because you believe you should be kind to others. It is not easy to believe in something and to always behave like you believe. Native people had strong beliefs. They tried to live their lives according to their beliefs. Like all people, sometimes they made mistakes, but they lived according to their beliefs.

Living Their Beliefs

Native people lived in open camps. There were no locks on their lodges or tipis. Native people had great honor. They believed it was wrong to take another person's property. There was little stealing in the camps of the native people.

Native people believed it was important to share with others. A good hunter always gave gifts to the poor of the tribe and to those who could not provide for themselves. An older person who could no longer hunt, for example, would be given meat and hides by the successful hunters.

Native people believed in being responsible. It was not easy to live in early Nebraska. Every day, native people had to be concerned about having enough food, having clothes, having fuel for fire, having water to use for cooking and drinking and many other things we take for granted today. If a tribe was going to exist, every person had to do his or her work.

In order to live, the work was divided by sex. Males hunted and butchered game. In the village tribes, males would clear the plots of land for planting the crops. The males would also cut and transport the logs to build the earth lodges. Males made weapons, stone tools, and did work with wood. Females were responsible for the preparation of all meals, the hauling of fuel and water, the dressing of skins and the making of all clothing, and for putting up and taking down the tipi. In the village tribes, females were responsible for planting and taking care of the crops. Females also dug roots and collected berries.

Children learned their jobs early in life. Usually children spent much time with their grandparents who taught them how they were to live. They learned the rules of the tribe and proper manners. When they played, young boys would go on pretend hunts or fight pretend battles while young girls built small tipis and played house. The parents of the native children were very loving. They seldom spanked their children. By the time children reached your age, around 10 years old, the girls played only with other girls and the boys played only with other boys. If a girl had an older brother, he would always be her "protector." He might tease his sister, but she was his responsibility to protect.

Girls learned from their grandmothers and mothers how to cook, treat hides, dig roots, and do all the other female chores. Boys learned from their fathers, uncles, and grandfathers how to care for the horses, make weapons, shoot, and hunt. Girls your age always had an escort. Usually the mother or the grandmother would go with a young girl who went to carry water or find fuel. Boys your age had much greater freedom to roam freely and to do many things. Regardless of sex, boys and girls quickly had to learn to be responsible. The future of the tribe was in their hands.

Heritage

The native people were a proud people. They were proud to be members of their tribes. They were proud of their family and their relatives. Unlike people today, native people could not write down their history because they had no written language. Instead there were certain people who were great storytellers. The storytellers had been taught stories by their elders about the tribe or about their family, and they would tell their stories for all to enjoy. As a storyteller grew old, he would teach a younger person the stories he knew. In this way the heritage of the tribe or the family was passed on over time.

Another way native people had of passing on their heritage was in their art work. Some tribes, particularly the Dakota tribes, kept buffalo hide calendars. The calendar hides were filled with pictures painted on the hide. The pictures told about important things that happened to the tribe over a period of years.

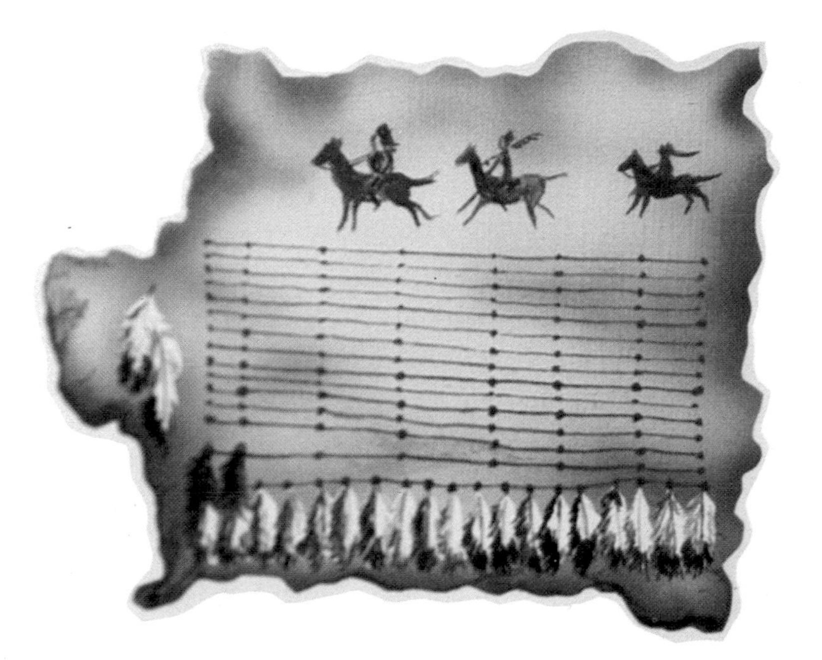

Calendar Hide

Many men painted pictures on their tipi covers which told stories about their brave deeds. Women usually painted patterns on clothing or bags. Women often did bead work where they made beautiful patterns (see pictures).

The holding of special ceremonies was another way the native people kept their heritage. In the Omaha tribe, for example, every spring after the first thunder was heard and the grass had begun to grow, a special ceremony was held. This ceremony was called "Turning the Child." The ceremony was for those young children who had begun to walk. When a child could walk without help, he or she was given a name and recognized as a member of the tribe. A special tent was set up. The child went into the tent for the "Turning the Child" ceremony. During the ceremony the child was turned to face the four directions: east, south, west, and north. Special songs were sung and the child was given a name along with a new pair of moccasins to begin his or her journey of life.

Through ceremonies like "Turning the Child," native people felt close to each other. They shared in these important ceremonies. Like stories, younger people were taught the tribal ceremonies so that the same ceremonies could be passed on forever. Even today, Native American people come together to sing and dance just like the people did in the Horse and Buffalo Culture. They do this to honor their past and to keep their heritage.

Food and Clothes

The buffalo was the most important resource for the people of the Horse and Buffalo Culture. The buffalo gave food, hides, bones, and other parts that were used by the native people. During the time of a hunt, native people ate much fresh meat. The people also had to find ways to keep the meat over a period of time. You have a refrigerator or freezer where your family now stores meat and other foods, but then the people had no electricity or modern machines so they used other ways to preserve and store food.

A favorite food used by the tribes in Nebraska was called pemmican (PEM-MI-CAN). In making pemmican (PEM-MI-CAN), native people would cut slices of buffalo meat. They dried the meat in the sun. After the meat was dried out, they pounded it with a stone tool until it became like meal. Then they mixed the pounded meat with melted fat and a paste made from crushed wild cherries. They stored pemmican in bags that could easily be carried.

Other foods enjoyed by the native people included fish, which were plentiful in the streams and rivers of Nebraska. Berries, such as choke-cherries, were picked in season. A prized food was the wild turnip. These plants were dug in the spring and early summer. They were usually peeled, sliced, and dried in the sun. The dried food was stored in bags and eaten in the winter. In the Sandhills of Nebraska, some tribes collected wild rice. In general, the native people were wise about how to find, prepare, and store many different kinds of food.

You have probably seen pictures of native people wearing colorful feathers with paint on their faces and bodies. Sometimes native people did dress in special clothes and paint their bodies in special ways. This was done for a reason, just as you and members of your family dress in special ways and wear jewelery or make-up to decorate your body. Normally, native people dressed in ordinary clothing. The clothes worn by the native people might look different from those you wear, but they served the same purposes.

Native clothing shows the great skill women had as clothes makers. In the winter native people often wore mittens, caps, moccasins, and warm robes that could also be used as blankets. In the summer native people wore breechcloths, dresses, moccasins, and shirts. It took skill, hard work, and time to make all the clothing worn by the native people.

The main resource for making clothes was the hide of animals, especially the buffalo. All animal hides were made ready for use by women. Depending on what was to be made, a hide was either tanned or used as tough rawhide.

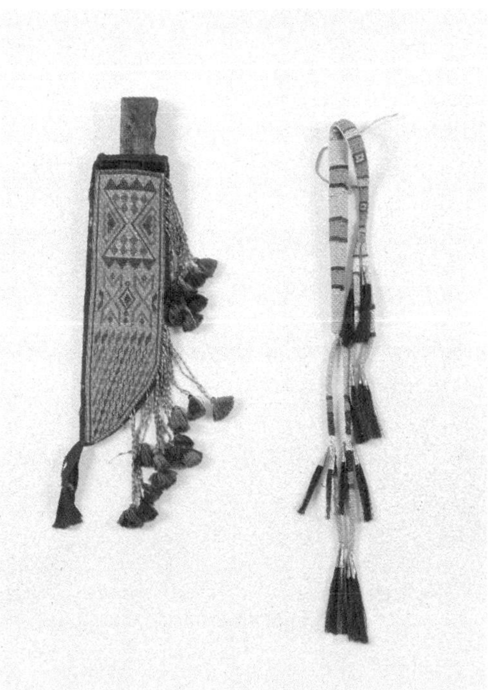

Photograph courtesy of the Nebraska Games and Parks Commission with Permission of Nebraska Historical Society

In working a hide, women would stake it to the ground with the hairy side down. They would scrape all the tissue from the hide with a scraper made of bone. Then they would put the hide in the sun to dry. After a few days the women would scrape the hide down to an even thickness. In order to make rawhide, they would remove all the hair with a bone tool. They used the rawhide to make containers, soles for moccasins, drums, rattles, bridles for horses, bindings, horse saddles, lariats, and other things.

Hides that were to be tanned were rubbed with an oil made from buffalo fat and animal brains. After the hide dried in the sun, it was rolled into a bundle. Later the hide was stretched and a rough edged stone was rolled over the hide. The hide was then worked until it became soft. For robes, the hair was left on the hide. For tanned hide, the hair was removed. Sometimes the hide was hung over a fire and smoked. The smoke helped the hide to remain soft. Tanned hides were used to make robes, tipis, moccasins, dresses, breechcloths, belts, bedding, bags of all sorts, and many other items.

Laws and Government

Whenever people come together, there has to be a set of rules (laws) which all must obey. The rule of law is based on the belief that each person gives up something and all people gain.

Can you find ways the rule of law affects your life? Here are some examples of what you might find.

Example #1—**No Running Near the Pool**

Have you ever been to a swimming pool that has a rule which says no running in the pool area? The reason for the rule is safety. Your safety and the safety of others. The pavement around a swimming pool is usually wet. Wet pavement is slippery. Each person who enters the pool area gives up the privilege of running while in the area. In this way, everybody that goes into the pool area is safer. Since nobody runs, there is less chance that people will slip and fall and less chance of injuries.

Example #2— **No Smoking in Theaters**

Smoking is a terrible habit, but many people smoke. To smoke or not to smoke is a personal matter. But, when it comes to smoking in a theater, there is a rule which forbids it. Smokers must give up their privilege of smoking so that they do not cause a fire. A fire in a theater could kill or injure many people. For the safety of all, no one is allowed to smoke in theaters.

In Nebraska today, we have elections in which the people of the state vote for persons who accept the responsibility for making laws for all of us. We call this "representative government." This means that persons voted into office represent the people.

The native people also had laws. Although their laws were not written down, the rule of law was important to every tribe. Persons were taught the laws of the tribe as they grew up. Any person who disobeyed the laws was punished. The most important laws dealt with the safety of the tribe.

Photograph courtesy of the Nebraska Unicameral Legislature Office

Members of the Nebraska Legislature meet every year in Lincoln to write laws for the people of Nebraska.

The native people did not elect persons to serve as their leaders. Instead, tribal leaders made themselves known to the people. A person became a tribal leader by his deeds. A man who was old enough to gain wisdom through his age, and who showed by his deeds over time that he was brave and generous, could become a tribal leader. In most tribes there was a group of wise, brave, and generous men who made decisions for the tribe. This group was called a council.

Warfare

Tribal groups in Nebraska and other places did make war against one another. The use of the horse gave all tribes greater mobility. This mobility meant that members from one tribe had a greater chance to meet members of another tribe. Frequently, tribes traded with one another and became friends. Sometimes the meetings were not so friendly. You already know that the Pawnee and the Apache fought against each other. The Pawnee and the Dakota were also bitter enemies.

Tribal warfare in Nebraska was fought with certain rules. The use of the horse brought "raid" warfare. A raid was when a small group of warriors attacked the camp of an enemy. A raid was often led by a man who was known for his bravery. Many times the raiders would steal the horses of an enemy since horses were so valuable. The tribe whose camp was being raided would fight to protect their property and lives. People were killed in these fights, but the bravest act a warrior could do was to touch an enemy with a special stick or a hand. This was known as a coup (KU). Coup is a French word which means to hit or to strike.

Through acts in war a man established his bravery. Men would tell stories at tribal gatherings about their deeds in battle. They would count coup. Stories of brave acts done in battle were often painted by men on their tipis and robes. Men also wore special feathers or animal tails and skins as signs of their deeds in battle.

The Horse and Change

How different life had become for people in Nebraska by the 1800's. The horse allowed people to move about freely. Even the village dwellers relied more completely on hunting the buffalo. As the people had more success in hunting the buffalo, they ate better and became richer. They became richer in the sense that they had bigger tipis, more horses, and more clothing. They made up rules about sharing their riches. Those who had more shared with those who had less. Rules were made up about the jobs males and females could do within the tribe. Special ceremonies and dances became important. Games were played, and music and art were shared by all. Sad as it may be, war also became a part of life in the Horse and Buffalo Culture.

Up to this time, the native people of Nebraska had little contact with white people. The native people had gotten horses because of the Spanish, and they had traded for guns and other goods with traders. The native people enjoyed their way of life. Some tribal holy men had said white people would come and bring great change. Most native people, however, thought life in the Horse and Buffalo Culture would never change.

Important Ideas to Remember from Life in the Horse and Buffalo Culture

All people share basic needs. People have need for food, clothing, and shelter.

People live together in groups to provide for their basic needs.

When people live together they have rules or laws which all must obey.

The rule of law is that each person in a group gives up some freedoms so that every person in the group is made safer.

People in groups form governments which make laws and protect the members of the group.

People in the Horse and Buffalo Culture in Nebraska lived together in tribal groups. Each tribal group had rules, beliefs, government, and leaders who helped provide for the needs of every person.

All tribal groups in the Horse and Buffalo Culture depended upon the buffalo as the most important resource.

All tribal groups in the Horse and Buffalo Culture depended upon the horse as the basic means of transportation to be used in hunting and war.

People in the Horse and Buffalo Culture honored the great life-giving force in the world, the Great Mystery.

The belief in the Great Mystery affected how people in the Horse and Buffalo Culture behaved.

People in the Horse and Buffalo Culture believed it was important for a person to be honest, responsible, and charitable.

People in the Horse and Buffalo Culture divided the work to be done according to sex. Males were responsible for certain jobs and females were responsible for certain jobs.

Children in the Horse and Buffalo Culture were taught by their grandparents, parents, relatives, and other elders.

People in the Horse and Buffalo Culture kept their heritage through their stories, their songs and dances, their ceremonies, and their art work.

Males in the Horse and Buffalo Culture fought in wars against members of other tribes.

Through warfare, males in the Horse and Buffalo Culture established their bravery.

A man in the Horse and Buffalo Culture had to be brave to be respected.

Things to Do

1. Guide words to good reading.

   NATIVE AMERICAN or INDIAN ART
   NATIVE AMERICAN or INDIAN STORIES or LEGENDS
   NATIVE AMERICAN or INDIAN DANCE
   OMAHA INDIANS or OMAHA TRIBE
   PEMMICAN
   COUP
   RAWHIDE
   TANNED HIDE
   LEGISLATURE

2. Use the guide words Native American Art or Indian Art. Go to your school or town library and find some examples of art work done by Native Americans, either past or present. Are there special things you notice about design and use of color? Create a painting in a Native American style. Native American art is part of our great heritage as Americans.
3. Here is a question for class discussion. Think about this question for awhile. Get some ideas down on paper and be ready to share your ideas with others as you listen to their ideas.

   What can we learn from the people who lived in the Horse and Buffalo Culture that we might use in our own lives today?

CHAPTER SEVEN
THE GREAT DESERT

What Is a Desert?

Have you ever heard of a desert? Geographers (GE-OG-RA-PHERS) are scientists who study about the earth. In studying the earth, geographers (GE-OG-RA-PHERS) have found there are some places on earth that receive little rainfall. Due to the lack of rain, these places usually have limited life—few plants and animals. Geographers call these places deserts.

Over time people have come to use the word desert to mean more than just an area that lacks rain. The word desert is sometimes used to describe a place that people think has little value. This was how many Americans viewed Nebraska in the early history of our country. They thought Nebraska was a useless place, a desert. They knew little about the native people or how the native people had lived as farmers and hunters in Nebraska for so many years. Once people discovered that Nebraska was a place of great promise, life in Nebraska changed quickly.

Early Explorers in Nebraska

You already know about the Europeans and why they came to America. (You might want to review Chapter 4.) On July 4, 1776, the thirteen English colonies along the Atlantic Coast issued the Declaration of Independence. This was the birthday of our country. After a long war with England, the thirteen colonies won their freedom from England. They agreed to become one country, the United States of America. The United States continued to grow as more people came from Europe and other places in the world. The western border of the United States was the Mississippi River (see map). The European countries that had set up colonies in America still owned much land.

In 1803, the President of the United States was Thomas Jefferson. President Jefferson agreed to buy a large piece of land called the Louisiana Territory from France. The Louisiana Purchase doubled the size of the United States. Nebraska was part of the Louisiana Purchase (see map).

Even though the United States now owned all the land in the Louisiana Territory, people knew little about the area. French and Spanish traders had worked in the area, but little information was written down. President Jefferson sent two men, Meriwether Lewis and William Clark, to explore the new territory. Jefferson told them he wanted to know about the land, the plants, and the animals they might find, and about the Indian people they would meet. Lewis and Clark led a group of forty-five people. They started out from St.Louis in May, 1804, and traveled up the Missouri River. By July, 1804, they had reached Nebraska. They found wild grapes, plums, and cherries along the river. In early August they held their first council with the native people of Nebraska at a place they called Council Bluffs near Ft. Calhoun.

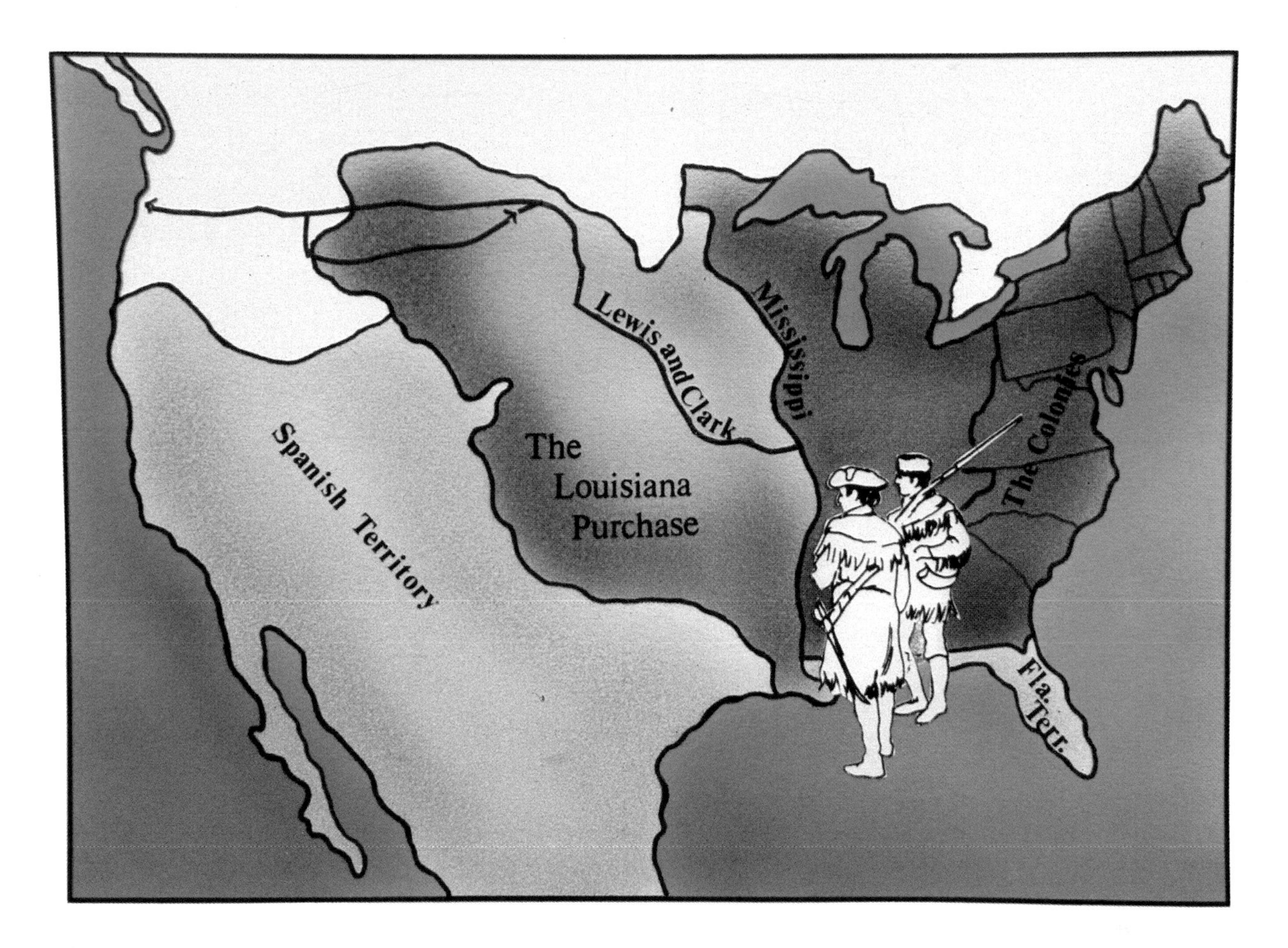

Journey of Lewis and Clark

In late August, Lewis and Clark camped in what is now Cedar County, Nebraska. Here they met with members of the Sioux nation. They continued up the river and met with members of the Ponca Tribe near where the Niobrara River runs into the Missouri River. The explorers traveled all the way to the Pacific Ocean and then returned to St. Louis. It took them over two years to complete their journey. They gave much information to the American people about the area they explored.

In July, 1806, a man named Zebulon Pike left St. Louis with a group of twenty-two men. They traveled west across Missouri and Kansas. Pike and his men also explored along the Republican River, which now marks the southern border of Nebraska. Pike continued west into Colorado and New Mexico. A famous mountain near Colorado Springs, Colorado is named in honor of Zebulon Pike. Do you know the name of that mountain?

A third explorer who came to Nebraska was sent by the American government in 1819. Major Stephen Long brought the first steamboat up the Missouri River to the Council Bluffs. In 1820, Major Long and twenty men began following the Platte River towards the west. After a few days they reached the Pawnee villages along the Loup River. They continued west towards the junction of the North and South Platte Rivers where they followed the South Platte River into Colorado. Long called the area west of the Missouri River the "Great American Desert." Long said the area would never be suited to farming.

The early explorers who were sent into the area wrote down much information. People today know more about what Nebraska was like in those days because of the written records made by the early explorers. Major Long's report, and the reports of others, led people to believe that no one would want to live in the area. For that reason, people did not want to move to Nebraska. Nebraska remained a place where the traders came to trade goods with the native people.

In the early history of our country, the United States Government sent explorers into the Louisiana Territory. Today the United States is sending explorers into space. The explorers who came to Nebraska in the early 1800's had to be brave people. They had to have much curiosity. They had to be people who used their five senses well so they could write down lots of information.

Do you think the space explorers of today are like the explorers who came to early Nebraska? Why or why not?

Why do you think human beings want to explore the unknown?

Traders

Long before the Louisiana Territory was sold to the United States, long before the explorers entered Nebraska, white people had come to the area. Fur traders from the European countries had traveled up the Missouri and Platte Rivers. The traders were interested in getting furs (animal pelts) from the native people. The traders offered the native people guns, cloth, knives, axes, beads, pots and pans, sugar, and many other goods in exchange for furs. The furs were taken back to a larger city like St. Louis on the Missouri River. The furs were then sold to companies who used the furs to make coats and hats.

Although the traders traded with the native people of Nebraska, they seldom made their permanent home in Nebraska. The goods they brought to the native people, however, caused great changes in how the native people lived. The native people wanted the goods the traders brought. Native men were willing to kill more animals than they needed in order to get goods from the traders. The guns and knives provided by the traders allowed native men to kill more animals. This meant that native women had to work harder to get the animal skins ready to trade. Life for the native people began to change.

The traders brought other things to the native people that introduced change. One item the native people had never used was whiskey. Whiskey is a dangerous drug. The traders found they could get many furs for a small amount of whiskey. Many traders had a problem with whiskey and the use of whiskey also became a serious problem for the native people. It made them sick, just as it does many people today.

Whiskey was not the only problem brought by the traders. New diseases, especially smallpox, were brought by the traders and others to Nebraska. The native people knew nothing about the new diseases. Once a person got sick, the disease spread to others. Great numbers of native people died due to the outbreak of disease.

After the United States bought Louisiana from France, traders continued to trade with the native people. Much of the trading took place west of Nebraska, but one important trading post was opened along the Missouri River. This post was called Bellevue. At the Bellevue trading post, people of the Omaha, Oto, and Pawnee tribes came to trade. Later, Bellevue was to become the first town in Nebraska.

Indian Country

In the early 1800's, Nebraska was the home of many native people. Few of the tribal groups knew anything about the Louisiana Purchase. Yet, the Louisiana Purchase was to be of great importance to the native people. The new owner of Nebraska sent explorers into the area. Traders entered Nebraska in greater numbers. Still, the people of the United States thought of Nebraska and the neighboring area as a useless place. People thought this whole area was a good place for the native people to live. As more white people came to the United States to live, they wanted to own the land east of the Mississippi River. They asked the United States Government to use its army to drive the native people west into the Louisiana Purchase Territory. The people of the United States came to call Nebraska, and much of the territory west of the Missouri River, "Indian Country." The Great American Desert was a place whites were willing to allow the native people to live.

Important Ideas to Remember from the Great Desert

Geographers call a place that has little rainfall and limited forms of life a desert.

People use the word desert to mean a place that has little value.

In the early history of the United States, Nebraska was considered to be a desert by many Americans.

Nebraska became a part of the United States through the Louisiana Purchase in 1803.

Meriwether Lewis, William Clark, Zebulon Pike, and Major Stephen Long were early explorers sent by the United States Government to explore the territory west of the Missouri River.

The early explorers recorded much information about early Nebraska.

Some of the early explorers led the American people to believe that Nebraska was a worthless desert.

White traders came to Nebraska to get furs from the native people.

The traders brought goods to the native people of Nebraska which caused great changes in the way native people lived.

The traders and others brought disease and whiskey to the native people which caused much sickness and death.

Bellevue was one important post opened by the traders along the Missouri River.

Bellevue was to become the earliest town in Nebraska.

In the early history of the United States, Nebraska was called Indian Country. White people thought Nebraska was a desert, a place where they were willing to allow the native people to live.

Things to Do

1. Guide words to explore.

   GREAT AMERICAN DESERT
   LOUISIANA PURCHASE
   THOMAS JEFFERSON
   LEWIS AND CLARK
   ZEBULON PIKE
   STEPHEN LONG
   FUR TRADE
   OTO TRIBE or OTO INDIANS
   BELLEVUE
   INDIAN TERRITORY

2. The Missouri, the Platte, and the Republican Rivers were important to the early explorers who came to Nebraska. Why do you think early explorers either traveled on or followed the rivers in their explorations?
3. Who do you think caused greater changes in early Nebraska, the explorers or the traders? Why?

CHAPTER EIGHT

HIGHWAY TO THE PROMISED LAND

The Grass Is Always Greener

Have you ever moved? Moving is no easy job. Packing all your belongings in boxes. Hoping that nothing breaks. Leaving friends and neighbors. Traveling to a new place. Hoping to find everything you think you packed. Making new friends and neighbors. Yet, there is a certain excitement about moving. It is a grand adventure.

Personal note from the author—When I was nine years old my family moved into a different house. It was a two-story house. I thought we were the richest people in the world. There were so many new places to explore in the house and around the neighborhood. I lived in that house until I finished high school and moved away from home. I often think about that house, and when I do, I feel happy and sad at the same time. Have you ever felt that way? Why do you think I feel that way about a house I lived in so long ago?

I think I know why.
They're still back there you know.
Smiling, laughing, crying.
I can't go back anymore.
But, I remember.

Do yourself a favor. Ask your parents to tell you about a move they'll never forget, or about their house of memories. I'll bet your teacher might like to share some stories with you too!

People often move because they think something better awaits them in a new place. Have you ever heard this expression? "The grass is always greener on the other side of the fence." For many Americans in the 1840's and 1850's, the grass looked greener on the other side of the country. The movement towards the Pacific Coast began with the fur traders moving into the Rocky Mountains. The European countries of England and Spain claimed they owned the land along the Pacific Ocean. They tried to keep the Americans out of their territory. Many Americans believed this territory belonged to the United States. In 1830, a group of fur traders found they could take wagons from Missouri to Wyoming. By using wagons they could haul many furs instead of the few furs they could take on small boats using the rivers. A short time later another group of Americans discovered you could

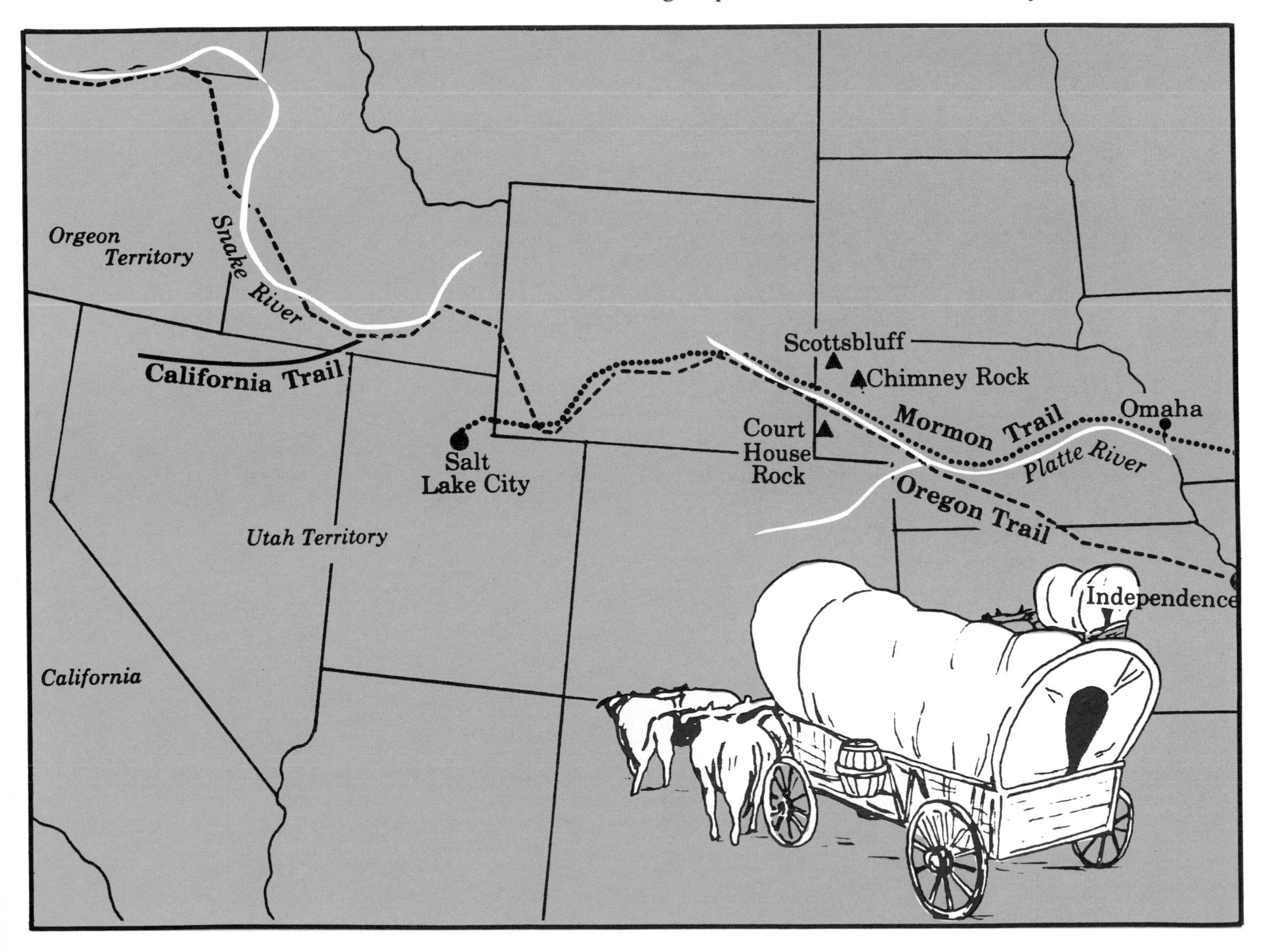

follow the same trail the fur traders used from Missouri across Indian Country into the mountains. They found it was possible to cross the mountains with wagons and travel to California and Oregon. This trail went across Nebraska and became known as the Oregon Trail. (See map. You can see that along the Snake River in Idaho a trail known as the California Trail broke off from the Oregon Trail.)

The Great Highway

Beginning in 1841, when a small band of people followed the Oregon Trail, through the 1850's, a steady stream of people made their way west each year. These were people looking for a better life in Oregon or California. They usually started out in Independence, Missouri near the present city of Kansas City. From Independence they headed northwest across a portion of Kansas and entered Nebraska near the Gage and Jefferson county lines. The trail followed the Little Blue River west into Adams County. Near the "Grand Island" in Hall County, travelers picked up the Platte River. They traveled west along the south side of the Platte River into Keith County, just east of Big Springs. Here the trail crossed over the South Platte and continued up the south side of the North Platte River past the famous landmarks Courthouse Rock, Jail Rock, Chimney Rock, and Scotts Bluff, west into Wyoming (see map).

The journey to Oregon or to California took many weeks. People would form a wagon train in Independence in the spring. The wagons were usually pulled by oxen and traveled about 15 miles per day. At that rate it took all summer to reach the Pacific Coast. People often got sick on the trail. Many died along the way.

Other things happened to cause people to want to move west. One group of people called the Mormons (members of a religious group called the Church of Jesus Christ of Latter Day Saints) were led by their leader, Brigham Young, to Nebraska in 1846. The Mormons were seeking to find a new home. Over 3,000 Mormon people made their "Winter Quarters" at Florence during the winter of 1846–47. Florence is located along the Missouri River on the north edge of Omaha. Here more than 600 Mormon people died during the harsh winter of 1846–47. Today the Mormon Cemetery remains as a beautiful place of rest for those who died at "Winter Quarters."

Photograph courtesy of the Nebraska State Historical Society

Chimney Rock and Scotts Bluff stood as important landmarks along the Oregon Trail.

Photograph courtesy of the Nebraska State Historical Society

In 1847, Brigham Young led a small group of Mormons to their new home in the Great Salt Lake Valley in Utah. The Mormons traveled along the north side of the Platte River from Douglas and Sarpy Counties west towards the place where the North and South Platte Rivers meet. The Mormons followed the North Platte River along the north side into Wyoming. As you can see on the map (refer to map on page 61), in western Wyoming the Mormons headed south into Utah and the Great Salt Lake Valley. This route became known as the Mormon Trail.

Photograph courtesy of Florence Historical Society
Church of Jesus Christ of Latter Day Saints

This beautiful Mormon Cemetery in the Florence area of Omaha is the final resting spot for many Mormons who died at Winter Quarters.

Photograph courtesy of Church of Jesus Christ Latter Day Saints

Mormon people used handcarts to haul their goods as they walked to "the Promised Land."

In 1848, Brigham Young led more than 2,000 followers to their new home at Salt Lake. Hundreds more came to Nebraska to start on their trip to the "Promised Land." Many arrived in Nebraska with few possessions and little money. They could not afford to buy wagons to haul their goods and families. The Mormon people were so determined to move west that in 1856 a group of 500 Mormons set out with handcarts. They placed a few goods and food in the carts and began walking to the Salt Lake Valley. More than 150 persons died in the 1856 attempt to push carts to the new Mormon home. This did not stop the Mormons. Between 1857 and 1860, over 3,000 Mormons walked to Salt Lake from Nebraska.

In 1849, thousands of people traveled west along the Great Platte Highway because of another promise, the promise of getting rich. In 1848, gold was discovered in California. Remember how the Spanish explorer Coronado (KOR-UH-NAH-DOH) came into the Great Plains area in 1542 seeking gold (see Chapter 4)? Throughout human history, gold has been valued. Whenever gold is discovered somewhere, people seem to get "gold fever." When gold was discovered in California, "gold fever" swept the country. Thousands of people traveled to California. In 1849, 30,000 people crossed Nebraska. In 1850, 50,000 people traveled along the Great Platte Highway.

The Great Platte Highway Today.

Now you know many people traveled the Great Platte Highway across Nebraska in the 1840's and 1850's. Do you think people still travel the same highway?

1. Find a highway map of Nebraska.
2. Trace, with your finger, the route of Interstate 80 across Nebraska.

If you want to know how many people use the Great Platte Highway (Interstate 80) today, here is what you can do. Write a letter to the Nebraska Department of Economic Development. Ask how many travelers have crossed Nebraska on Interstate 80 during the past year. You might also ask the Department of Economic Development to send you information about things to see and do along the Great Platte Highway.

Nebraska Department of Economic Development
Division of Tourism and Travel
Nebraska State Office Building
301 Centennial Mall, South
Lincoln, Nebraska 68509

Forts and Treaties

Nebraska was part of Indian Country, the land given over to the native people. You know how the native people lived in Nebraska during the Horse and Buffalo Culture. In dealing with early traders, the native people had few fears. The traders brought change to the Horse and Buffalo Culture, but there were not many white people in Nebraska. As white people started using the Great Platte Highway to travel west, the first serious troubles started between whites and the native people. The trouble lasted for nearly fifty years and is one of the saddest parts of Nebraska's story.

The Platte River Valley was in the middle of buffalo country. The white people who traveled along the Great Platte Highway thought that the land belonged to the people of the United States. After all, the United States bought the land from France. The native people viewed the land as a hunting area. They knew nothing about the ownership of land. They had long hunted buffalo in the area. As more whites passed through Nebraska, they killed buffalo along the way. The cattle and horses of the white people ate the grass in the Platte Valley. This grass had been a source of food for the buffalo. Soon the buffalo herds left the Platte River Valley. The buffalo were important to the native people, especially to the nomadic tribes of western Nebraska. Hunters from the Dakota, Cheyenne, and Arapaho Tribes were angry about the buffalo leaving the Platte Valley. Sometimes small bands of native people would surround and attack a party of white travelers. The frightened whites thought all native people were dangerous. Some whites would shoot at native people for no reason.

White people wanted to travel the Great Platte Highway in safety. Soon they demanded that the United States Government protect them. In 1848, the government built a fort on the Platte River near the present town of Kearney. Fort Kearny housed soldiers who were to protect white travelers along the Great Platte Highway. In 1849, the government took over a fur trading post in Wyoming. This post became known as Fort Laramie. It was another place to put soldiers along the Oregon and Mormon Trails to protect white travelers.

In 1851, the Government of the United States called for a great peace meeting. The government invited people from all the tribes in the region. The meeting was held in what is now Scotts Bluff County. Here, nearly 10,000 native people gathered. The government wanted to make a treaty (an agreement) with the native people. The native people were to promise that they would not attack whites traveling along the Great Platte Highway. The government promised to set up boundaries where each tribe could hunt freely. In Nebraska, the Western Dakota were promised all the land north of the North Platte River. The Cheyenne and Arapaho were promised all the land south of the North Platte River. The government also promised to give the native people $50,000 in food and goods every year for fifty years.

Promises Never Kept

The agreement made at the great peace meeting is called the Treaty of Fort Laramie of 1851. Neither the white people nor the native people kept the promises they made in the agreement. The Treaty of Fort Laramie was like many other agreements made between the whites and the native people, promises were broken and people were killed. Why do you think that happened? Think about that question. Before you finish this chapter, write down some reasons you think the promises were rarely kept between the white and native people.

Ignorance, Attitude, and Pride

Have you ever heard the word ignorant (IG-NO-RANT)? Ignorant means to have little knowledge. Maybe you have heard someone say, "I don't know anything about cars." What that person may be saying is that he/she has little knowledge about how automobiles work. Perhaps that person could not fix a car in need of repair because of a lack of knowledge. Would you want a person ignorant about automobiles to work on your family's car? Probably not!

When it came to agreements between the white and native people, ignorance was the greatest problem. Neither group of people knew much about the other. Most whites knew nothing about the culture of the native people. Since they knew nothing about the native people, they had no respect for the beliefs and the life styles of the different tribal groups. The native people were equally as ignorant about the whites.

Another problem was attitude. How you feel about another person influences how you behave towards that person. This is called attitude. Most white people held the attitude that native people had no rights except those rights given to them by the whites. The native people complained at the great peace meeting of 1851 that the whites had driven the buffalo out of the Platte Valley. They complained that the whites had brought diseases. They complained about the destruction of the grass and the trees in the Platte Valley. The whites paid no attention to those complaints. The whites held the attitude that the native people had no right to complain.

On the other hand, there were native leaders who made promises to the whites that could never be kept. You know that a council of wise men often made decisions for tribal groups in the Horse and Buffalo Culture. The whites, because of their ignorance, thought a single chief or leader could make a promise for an entire tribe. Many tribal members refused to obey promises made by a single leader. This often led to disagreements between whites and the native people.

You probably feel your school is a good school, and you are happy to be a student there. You might even think your school is better than other schools. What you feel about your school is pride. It is fine to have pride in your school, your family, or yourself. Pride can be bad when you begin to think you are better than others. When you feel that way, you treat others as if they are less important than you.

Both the whites and the native people were proud. At times, they tended to treat each other in ways that showed they did not respect each other. When you add ignorance, attitude, and pride together, you find strong reasons why the two groups did not keep their promises to one another. When they failed to keep their promises, war broke out. It is sad to know that many people were killed in Nebraska during these wars. If there is ever to be peace amongst people, it may help to think about why these terrible wars happened in Nebraska at this time. Are there things you can do to be a person of peace?

The Road to Change

The Great Platte Highway was more than an important road. It brought great numbers of white people to Nebraska. Use of the Great Platte Highway helped lead to the beginning of the so called "Indian Wars," a period of time in which white and native people fought each other. When the wars ended, the buffalo were destroyed. The native people were defeated and made to live in special areas called "reservations." The road to all these changes in Nebraska began on the Great Platte Highway.

Important Ideas to Remember from Highway to the Promised Land

Many Americans moved west into the Rocky Mountain area and the Pacific Coast during the 1840's and 1850's.

Americans moved west during this time to seek a better life. Some wanted to find new land in Oregon or California. Some wanted to find gold in California. Some wanted to find a new place to live according to their religious beliefs.

Two of the most important routes people followed in traveling west were the Oregon Trail and the Mormon Trail.

Both the Oregon and Mormon Trails followed the Platte River through Nebraska.

The Platte River Valley became the great highway to a new promised land in the west during the 1840's and 1850's.

The Platte Valley was an important buffalo hunting area to the native people of Nebraska.

The large number of white travelers going across Nebraska in the 1840's and 1850's drove the buffalo herds out of the Platte Valley.

The need to use the Platte Valley by both the native people and the white people at this time led to conflict.

The United States Government put soldiers in forts along the Platte Valley to protect the white travelers using the Oregon and Mormon Trails.

The Government of the United States called for a big peace meeting in 1851. All tribal people in the area were invited to the meeting which was held in Scotts Bluff County, Nebraska.

An agreement called the Treaty of Fort Laramie of 1851 was made at the meeting between the Government of United States and tribal leaders. The agreement was to bring peace between the whites and the native people.

The Treaty of Fort Laramie failed to bring peace.

Ignorance, Attitude, and Pride led to continued war between the white and native people.

Use of the Great Platte Highway began the movement of many white people to Nebraska.

Use of the Great Platte Highway marked the beginning of the end for the Horse and Buffalo Culture in Nebraska.

Things to Do

1. Guide words to the Promised Land. Reading is the one way to fight ignorance.

   OREGON TRAIL
   MORMON TRAIL
   CALIFORNIA TRAIL
   BRIGHAM YOUNG
   GOLD RUSH
   FORT KEARNY
   FORT LARAMIE
   TREATY OF FORT LARAMIE

2. How close are you to the Oregon and Morman Trails in Nebraska? If possible, you may want to plan a trip with your teacher to some place or places along these historic trails. Use a map of Nebraska and locate the places that may be closest to you. Whether it be the Mormon Cemetery in the east or Scotts Bluff in the west, it is exciting to see these places where history was made.

   If travel is not possible for you, write to the Nebraska State Historical Society, to your local library, and to the Nebraska Game and Parks Commission asking for information about places along the Great Platte Highway.
3. Pretend you are a traveler along the Oregon Trail in the 1840's or 1850's. You are writing a letter to your friends who live back east. What will you tell them?
4. Pretend you are a tribal hunter in the Platte Valley during the 1840's or 1850's. You see an endless number of wagons carrying white travelers each day. Write down your feelings about what you see happening.

CHAPTER NINE
SLAVERY AND RAILROAD

The Shame of Slavery

While thousands of people moved west along the Great Platte Highway in the 1840's and 1850's, other things were happening in the United States that also affected Nebraska. Slavery was an issue that affected Nebraska.

Have you ever heard of slavery? It is not easy to understand slavery. Slavery means one group of people has control over another group of people. In slavery, people own people! Just as you may own a pet, a slave owner owned another human being. Over the long course of human history many different peoples have been enslaved. People of all races and colors have been forced into slavery. When slavery was brought to the United States, black people were used as slaves. The black slaves had no freedom. They were not allowed to go to school or to become educated. The slaves were made to work hard. They had to obey their owners or they were punished.

Slaves were brought to the United States from Africa. In Africa, black people lived in tribal groups much like the native people of Nebraska. White slave catchers would go to Africa (see map) and hunt down black tribal people. The slave catchers would put the black people in chains and brand

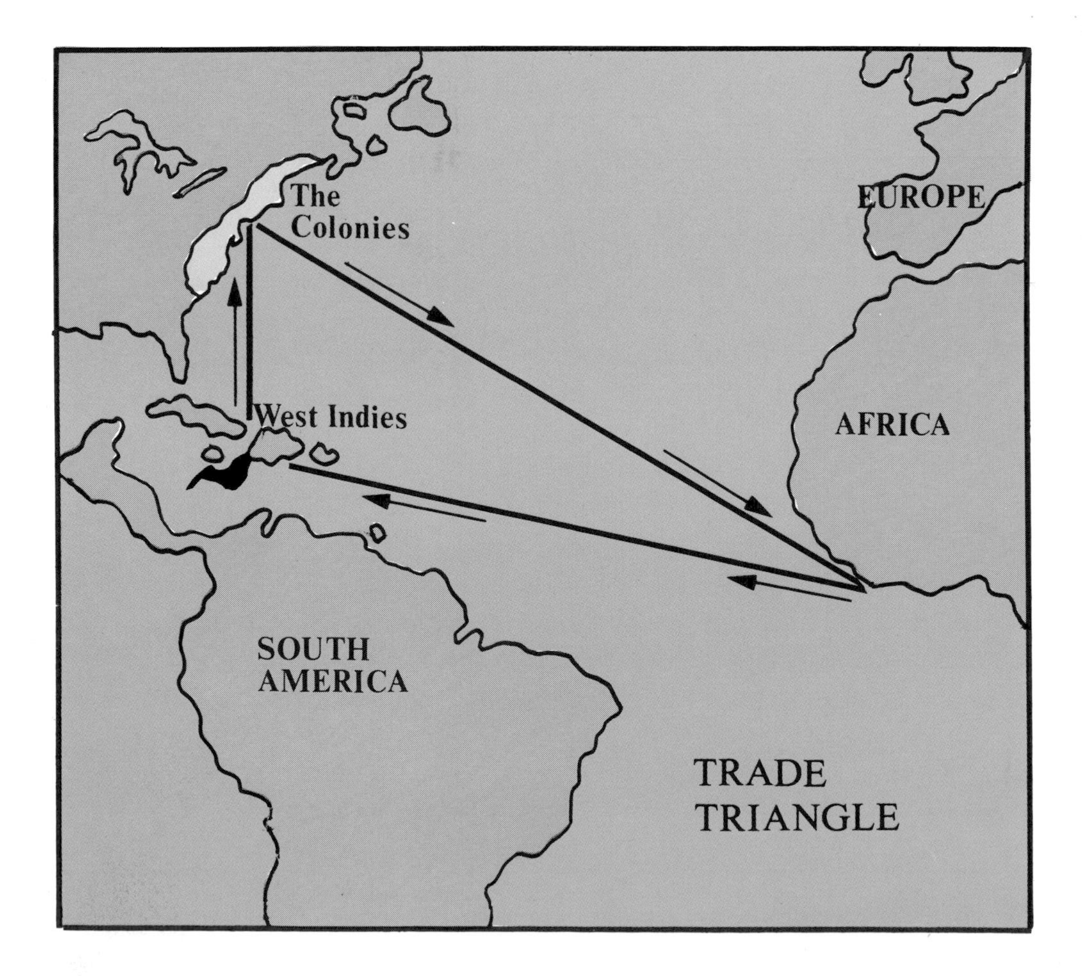

them like cattle. Then they took the captured black people on ships across the ocean and sold them to white slave owners in the United States.

Over time, slavery was only allowed in the southern United States (see map). White land owners in the south had big farms called plantations. The southern land owners grew crops like cotton, rice, and tobacco on the plantations. They had few machines, so they used the black slaves to do all the work.

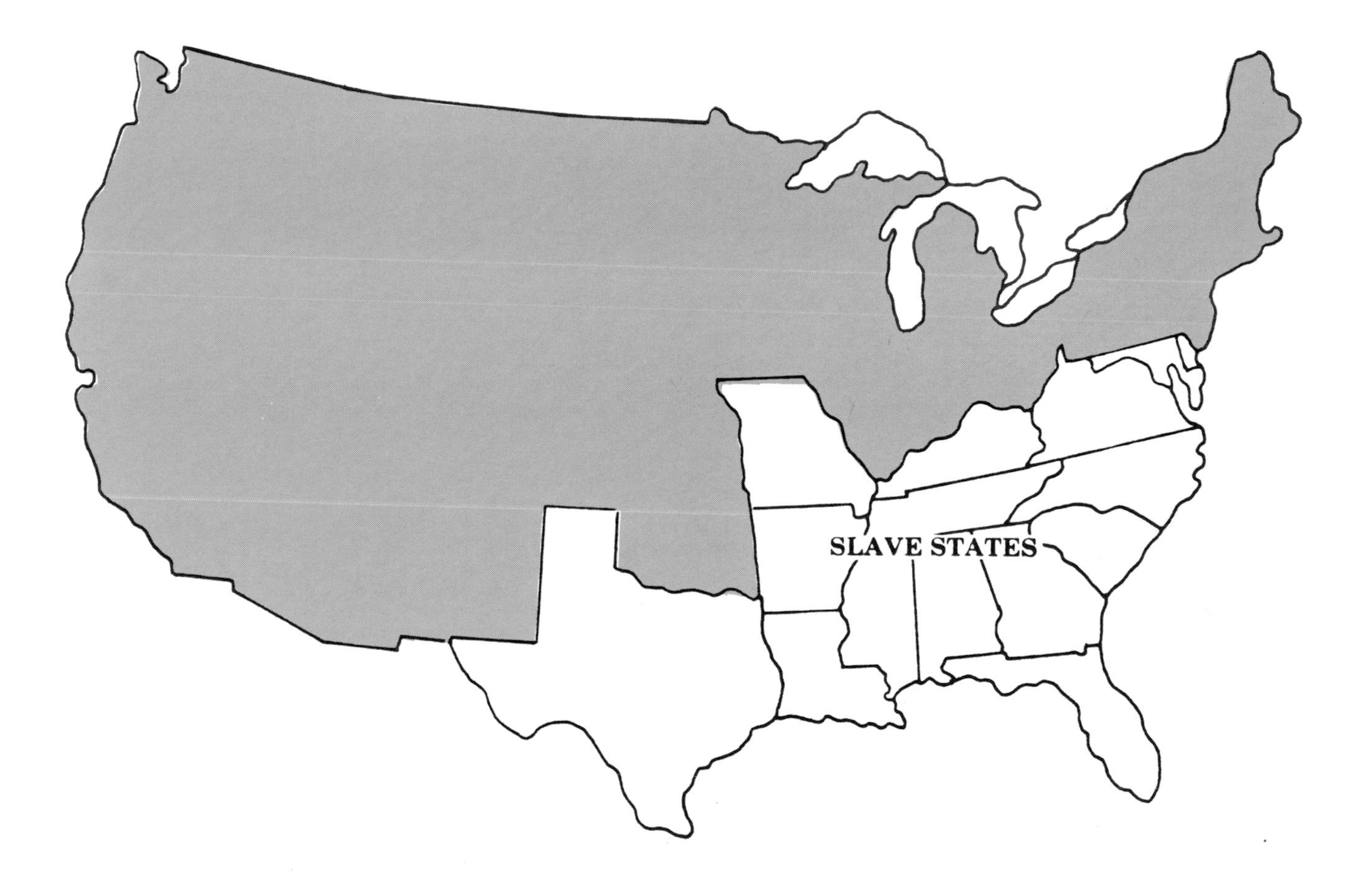

There were many white people who thought slavery was bad. These people did not want slavery to be allowed outside of the South. As people in the United States moved west across the Missouri River, the question of slavery was raised. Should people be allowed to take slaves into the new territory? Slave owners said that slaves were property— something a person owns. The slave owners believed they should be allowed to take their slaves anywhere they wanted. Those people against slavery said that slavery was evil. They believed it was wrong for one human being to own another person. Those against slavery did not want slavery to spread to other places in the United States.

Something to Think About

1. The chart on the next page lists eight items. Think about each item, and on a piece of paper rate the importance of the item to you. For example, are your parents Very Important, Important, Somewhat Important, or Not Important to you?
2. Find out how your classmates rated each item. Perhaps your teacher will record on the chalk board how the class rated each item.
3. Hold a class discussion about why the class rated the items the way they did.
4. Think about this in your discussions:

In slavery, the white slave catchers and slave owners did not care how black people felt about their families. Captured blacks in Africa were taken away from their families and friends. They were taken to a strange place never to see their families and friends again. In the United States slaves were bought and sold. Sometimes a child was sold and taken from his/her parents. Sometimes parents were sold and taken from their children.

During slavery days in the South it was against the law for slaves to be educated. Slave owners thought if slaves could read and write they might become disobedient. They wanted to keep the slaves ignorant.

Slaves had no right to make choices for themselves. They could not choose what kind of work they wanted to do. They could not choose where to live. They had no right to travel without the permission of their owner.

Slavery means a person is treated without respect. Slaves were not treated as though they were human beings. They were treated as though they were "things" that had no feelings and no intelligence.

Since slaves were not treated with respect, they were never rewarded for their efforts or talents. Slave owners used the talents and efforts of their slaves.

	Very Important	Important	Somewhat Important	Not Important
My Parents				
My Family				
Receiving an Education				
Freedom to Make Choices				
Freedom to Travel				
Being Treated With Respect				
Being Rewarded for My Efforts				
Being Rewarded for My Talents				

The slavery issue, as you will see, did affect Nebraska. For now, the important question for you to think about is why slavery was ever created. Why did people want to make slaves out of other people? Here is another important question for you to think about and discuss. What can you and your classmates do to treat each other with respect? We no longer have slavery in the United States, where one person owns another person. But, if people do not show respect towards one another, do we have slavery of another kind? In order to end slavery of any kind, what rights belong to every person as a human being? Make a list.

What must you do to make sure all of us, you and everyone else, maintain their rights as a human being?

Transcontinental Railroad

One thing Americans in the 1840's and 1850's seemed to agree on was the need for a railroad to cross the country. You can understand why a railroad would be important. Many people had moved west to California, Oregon, and Utah. People did not like to travel by wagon. It took a long time to cross the country. It was not comfortable and it was dangerous. A railroad line would allow people to cross the country quickly and safely. It would also allow people to ship and receive goods easily.

There were arguments about where a transcontinental (TRANS-CON-TI-NEN-TAL) railroad (a railroad that crosses the country) should be built. People in the South wanted the railroad built across the southern United States. People in the North wanted the railroad built across the northern United States. There were people who thought the railroad should be built along the Great Platte Highway. The Platte Valley had been a good route for travelers to follow.

If a railroad was to be built along the Platte Valley, some problems had to be settled. The Platte Valley was in the middle of Indian Country. Many tribal groups had been moved into Indian Country by the United States Government. If a railroad was to be built along the Platte Valley there would have to be further agreements, like the Treaty of Fort Laramie of 1851, with the native people. One way to deal with the problem of Indian Country was for the United States Government to make agreements with the native people and then to tell white people they could move to Nebraska and other places. The whites would be allowed to buy land, build houses, and use the land for farming.

If the United States Government invited white people to move to Indian Country, what about the question of slavery? Should people be allowed to bring slaves into Indian Country? Those who believed slavery to be evil said no slaves should be allowed in the newly opened territory. Those who favored slavery said slavery should be allowed anywhere. If people could not agree about slavery, they could not agree to build a railroad across the country.

In 1854, a law was made which is called the Kansas-Nebraska Act. This law set up two territories (see map). You can see that the Nebraska Territory was large. All or parts of the states of Nebraska, South Dakota, North Dakota, Colorado, Wyoming, Idaho, and Montana were a part of the Nebraska Territory. Treaties made with the native people after the Kansas-Nebraska Act gave ownership of most of the land in Indian Country to the United States Government. Some of this was land once promised to the native people. The government told white people they could move into the territories of Kansas and Nebraska to live. The government also said people living in Kansas and Nebraska could decide whether or not they wanted slavery. Now it was possible to build the transcontinental (TRANS-CON-TI-NEN-TAL) railroad through the Platte Valley.

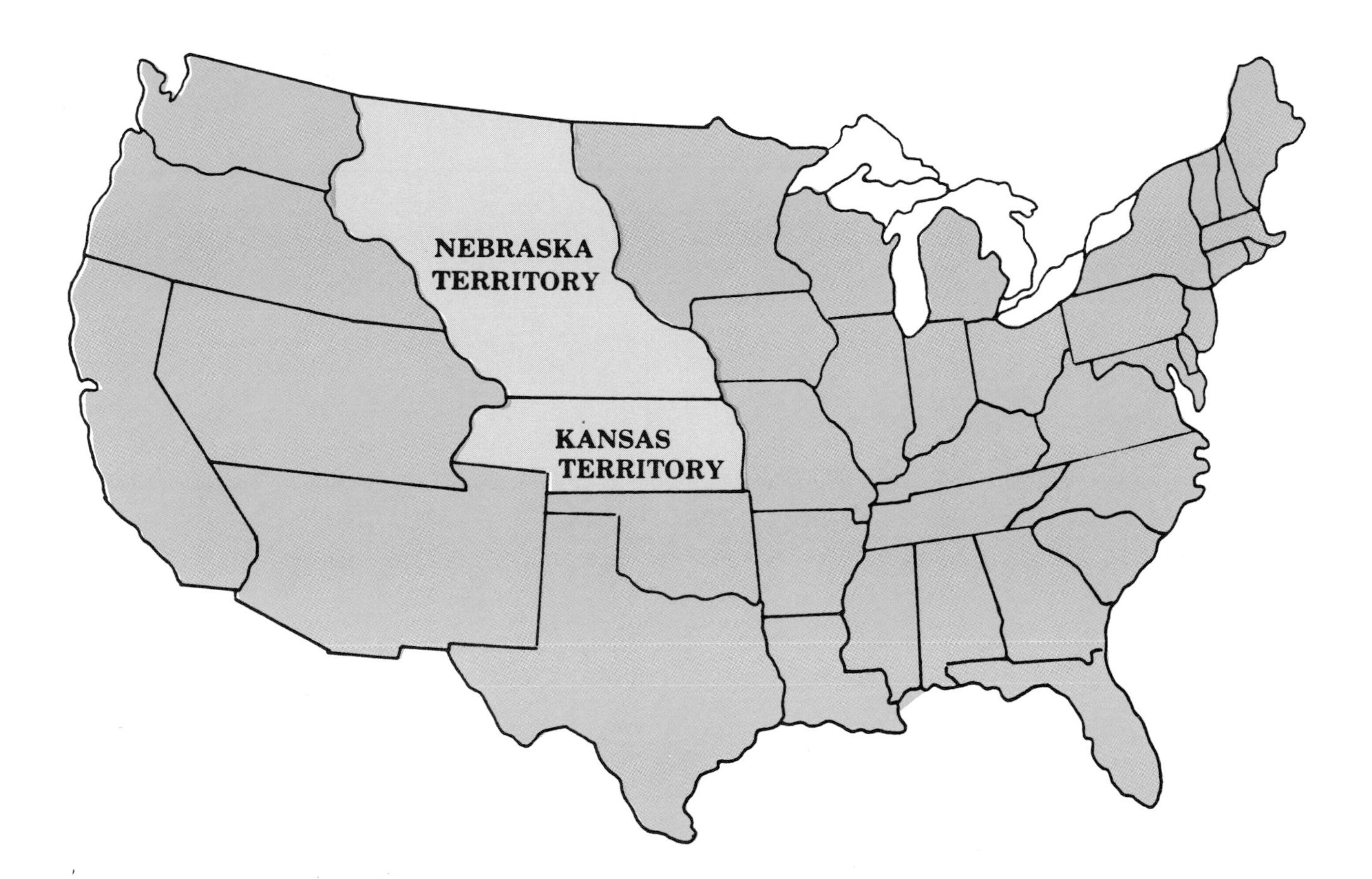

The Land is Plenty

A railroad is a means of transportation, a way to haul people and goods. It was the desire of the American people to build a railroad across the country that led to one of the most important changes in Nebraska's story. Nebraska, a land set aside for the native people, became part of an important railroad route. As part of the railroad route, Nebraska was opened for settlement. There was only one great problem that had to be solved before many settlers came to Nebraska. It was the problem of slavery. In 1861, a terrible war broke out between the states of the North (the Union) and the states of the South (the Confederacy). The Civil War lasted until April, 1865. When the war ended, slavery ended. With the end of slavery, people began moving across the Missouri River to Nebraska. The wealth that called people to Nebraska was not furs or gold, but the land. Nebraska began the change from Indian Country to farm and ranch country. The land that had been shaped by the forces of nature millions of years ago, the land that had supported the buffalo and made possible the Horse and Buffalo Culture, the rich land of Nebraska now called to people from all parts of the world. Like people over thousands of years had found, in Nebraska the land is plenty.

Important Ideas to Remember from Slavery and the Railroad

Slavery means that one group of people own and control another group of people.

In the early history of the United States, black people were made slaves.

Over time slavery was allowed only in the southern United States.

In the 1840's and 1850's Americans wanted to build a railroad across the United States.

The Platte Valley through Nebraska was thought to be a good route for a railroad.

The United States Government made agreements with the native people to take most of the land in Indian Country.

The United States Government made a law called the Kansas-Nebraska Act which created two large territories in what had been Indian Country.

White Americans were invited to move to Kansas and Nebraska, buy land, build homes, and use the land for farming.

The white people in the new territories of Kansas and Nebraska were to vote whether or not they would allow slavery in the territories.

Before many settlers came to Nebraska, a great war broke out in 1861 between the states of the North and the states of the South.

The Civil War ended in 1865. The South was defeated and slavery was ended.

With the end of the Civil War, Nebraska began to attract many settlers.

The railroad made it easier for people to come to Nebraska, and the rich land was available for those who wanted to farm.

Things to Do

1. Guide words that will open new territories for you.

   SLAVERY
   SLAVE TRADE ROUTE
   PLANTATION
   TRANSCONTINENTAL RAILROAD
   KANSAS-NEBRASKA ACT
   CIVIL WAR

2. One of the saddest things about slavery was that some people could never completely use their talents and abilities. As a human being, each of us is special. When we fail to respect the "specialness" in others, we fail to respect ourselves. Here is an opportunity for you. Take time to celebrate you! That's right, celebrate the fact that you are a human being with special gifts and talents. Use your imagination to create something that makes a statement about you. Share your creation with your classmates. You might even decorate your classroom with your creations. Let your creations say that "our classroom appreciates every person who shares and learns here."

CHAPTER TEN
STATEHOOD AND SETTLEMENT

Joining the Group

Are you a member of the 4-H Club, the scouts, or a youth group? If you are, you know about joining a group. In joining a group you share things in common with all the other members. As a group member, you accept the basic goals and rules of the group. A 4-H member, for example, pledges "to make the best better" by clear thinking, good health, and greater loyalty and service to others. The goals of 4-H include self improvement and the betterment of others. Each 4-H member remains an individual but joins with others to work for worthy goals.

In American history, when a territory became a state it was called joining the Union. Becoming a state was much like a person joining a group. A person who wants to join a group must make application to the group for membership. The application may be accepted by the group with certain conditions. The individual may have to pay dues, attend meetings, complete projects, and do other things to be a member. In joining the Union, a territory made application to become a state to the Congress of the United States. Territories making application to become states promised to obey the laws of the United States Government. Much like a person joining a group, states joining the Union kept their identity. Each state has land, a capital city, a government to make laws, and schools to educate young people.

When states joined the Union they did agree to give certain powers to the Government of the United States. It would be silly if every state had its own money. Nebraska money could not be spent in Colorado! When states joined the Union they agreed that only the Government of the United States could issue money. The dollar is a unit of money that can be spent in any state. The states agreed that it was the job of the United States Government to protect all the people from any enemy. There is one army, the United States Army, instead of 50 different armies. Although the states have given up some powers in joining the Union, they have kept other powers. State governments have many laws which protect their citizens. In the United States there are two levels of government, federal and state. The Government of the United States (federal government) protects and serves all the citizens of the country. The governments in the fifty states (state government) protect and serve all the citizens of their state. There are also county and local governments within the states. County and local governments are really part of the state government. Through laws, state governments give certain powers to county and local governments. This system of government is called federalism (FED-ER-AL-ISM).

Thinking About Federalism

Federalism (FED-ER-AL-ISM) is like a two-layer cake. The lower layer is made up of fifty parts, the fifty state governments. The upper layer is the Government of the United States. The Government of Nebraska is part of the lower layer. The Government of Nebraska serves and protects the people of Nebraska.

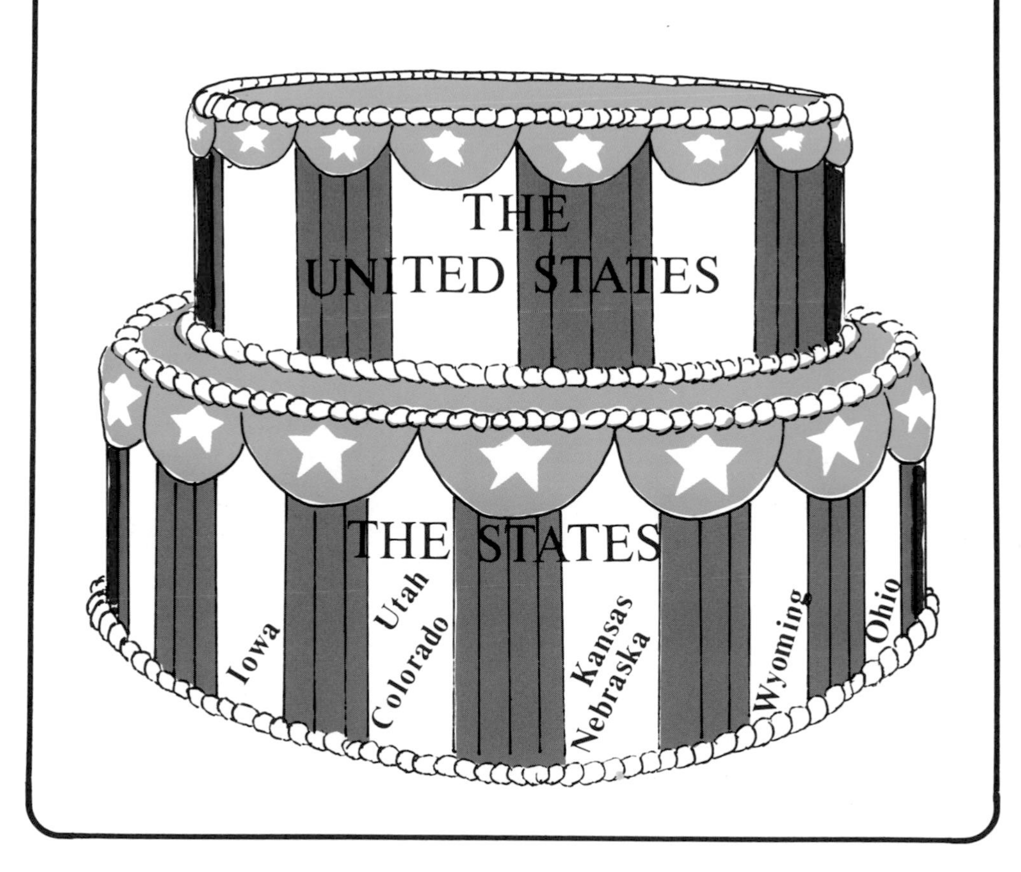

Listed below you will find some things that government does to protect and serve the people. On a piece of paper mark for each item whether you think the item belongs in the lower layer or the upper layer of the federalism cake. Tell why you made your choice.

1. Hire police officers and fire fighters to protect the people in Lincoln.
2. Build schools and hire teachers to educate young people in McCook.
3. Stop criminals from entering the United States.
4. Check theaters in Omaha to make sure they are safe for people.
5. Provide information about weather conditions across the United States.
6. Plow snow off Nebraska Interstate Highway 80 during the winter.
7. Require pets in Norfolk to have a license.
8. Set speed limits for automobile traffic in Chadron
9. Send astronauts into space.
10. (Here's a hard one, think carefully.) Prevent air pollution.

Did you know that government did so much to serve and protect the people? You can find out more about the responsibilities of government. Ask your parents to list what they must do to own and operate an automobile. Ask your teacher what he/she must do in order to teach in your school. Ask your principal what rules the school must meet in order to operate. As you ask about these things, do not forget to ask why the government makes such rules. Does it have something to do with protecting the people of the state?

By the way, what did you decide about air pollution (number 10 above)? Air does not remain in one place. As a matter of fact, the air over your community today may be over a community in Iowa tomorrow. The Government of the United States sets rules about air pollution. It is a problem that affects all the people in the United States.

Early Settlement

Now that you know about federalism (FED-ER-AL-ISM), you can understand what happened when Nebraska became a state. The huge territory of Nebraska had been created through the Kansas-Nebraska Act of 1854. The Government of the United States signed treaties with the native people and settlers began to move into the Nebraska Territory.

The Missouri River had long been a route followed to Nebraska. The early fur traders had used the Missouri River and so had Lewis and Clark. When people came to settle in the Nebraska Territory, they settled first along the Missouri River. The earliest towns in Nebraska were towns along the river. Bellevue (the old fur trading post), Nebraska City, Plattsmouth, Florence, and Omaha were important river towns. Omaha became the first capital city for the Nebraska Territory. A brick capitol building located near the Missouri River was built in Omaha in 1854.

Photograph courtesy of the Nebraska State Historical Society

First Capitol

Photograph courtesy of the Nebraska State Historical Society

When the Central Pacific and Union Pacific Railroads met at Promontory Point in 1869, the first transcontinental railroad was complete. The event was celebrated by driving the last spike, a golden spike, to hold the rails.

Other railroads were to follow. The Burlington Railroad began construction in Nebraska along the south side of the Platte Valley starting at Plattsmouth in 1869. The railroads played an important role in bringing many new settlers to Nebraska.

Statehood

The Nebraska Territory, as set up in the Kansas-Nebraska Act, did not remain the same. Gold was discovered in the Nebraska Territory in 1858. The discovery of gold in the Rocky Mountain area of what is now Colorado led to a gold rush much like the gold rush to California in 1849. So many people went to Colorado in search of gold that the Colorado Territory was created by the United States Government in 1861. The Dakota Territory was also carved out of the Nebraska Territory in 1861. In 1863, creation of the Idaho Territory took another hunk of Nebraska Territory.

Regardless of the loss of land, the Homestead Act, the end of the Civil War, and the building of the railroads all meant that more people would come to the Nebraska Territory. In 1866, people in the Nebraska Territory voted to join the Union and to ask that Nebraska become a state. The boundaries for Nebraska were fixed much as you know them today. Nebraska became a state on March 1, 1867, but there was one last issue to be settled. The territorial capital had been Omaha. Settlers living on the south side of the Platte River wanted a new location for the capital. After Nebraska became a state, a special group was named to study where Nebraska's new capital should be located. The group recommended that the new capital be located in the small town of Lancaster. The name of the town was changed to Lincoln, and a new capitol was built in 1868.

Growing Pains

In the first chapter you were asked to find some pictures of yourself and your family and to look at the changes that had taken place over time. There is a period of time in human life when change comes very rapidly. This is the period of infancy and youth. You can see from your family pictures how quickly you changed from being a baby to growing into a young child. Your body will continue to make rapid changes until you reach young adulthood.

The same thing happened to Nebraska once it became a territory. While Nebraska remained part of Indian Country, things were slowly changing. The movement of people towards the west and the use of the Platte Valley as a highway began a period of fast change. In a period of fourteen years, 1854-1868, Nebraska became first a territory and then a state; the native people were placed on reservations and could no longer freely hunt on the land; thousands of settlers came to Nebraska to farm and bought cheap land or received free land through the Homestead Act; after Nebraska became a state, the state capital was moved from Omaha to Lincoln.

Sometimes when your body goes through a rapid period of growth, you might feel discomfort. Bones and muscles are growing and you seem to ache. These types of pains are called "growing pains." The rapid changes of moving from Indian Country to territory to state brought some growing pains for Nebraska. You'll read about those growing pains in the chapters ahead. For now, it is well to remember another truth about change. Any time there is rapid change that involves people, there will also be some pain. Why do you think that is true?

Important Ideas to Remember from Statehood and Settlement

The United States of America has a federal system of government.

Federalism means there are two levels of government. One level of government is state government. Each of the fifty states has a state government. State governments protect and serve the people within their borders. A second level of government is federal or national government. The Government of the United States protects and serves all the American people.

After the Nebraska Territory was created through the Kansas-Nebraska Act, settlers came to Nebraska.

The first settlers lived along the Missouri River, and the earliest towns in Nebraska were established along the Missouri River.

Omaha became the capital city in Nebraska Territory.

Many settlers came to Nebraska to obtain land and to begin farming.

The Government of the United States sold land cheaply and even gave land to settlers who were willing to farm.

As railroads were built in Nebraska, more settlers were brought to the state.

Nebraska became a state on March 1, 1867.

After Nebraska became a state, the city of Lincoln was named the new state capital.

Things to Do

1. Our reading list continues to grow. Select a guide word and head for the nearest library.

   FEDERALISM
   FEDERAL UNION
   STATES
   GOVERNMENT OF THE UNITED STATES
   NEBRASKA TERRITORY
   HOMESTEAD ACT OF 1862
   UNION PACIFIC RAILROAD
   CENTRAL PACIFIC RAILROAD

GOLDEN SPIKE
PROMONTORY POINT
BURLINGTON RAILROAD
OMAHA, NEBRASKA
LINCOLN, NEBRASKA

2. During this chapter you have read about federalism. You may have discovered that government is important in our lives. As a class, write a letter to the Governor of Nebraska. Ask the Governor to explain to you what he/she thinks are the most important responsibilities that the Government of Nebraska has in protecting and serving the citizens of Nebraska.
3. Project Research. Hopefully, you have been discovering how much information you can find in using your library. Here is a challenge for you. You should be able to find a chart in your library that lists all the states and the order in which they entered the Union. The same chart will probably have information about each state. It will probably identify the capital for each state, give a recent state population figure, and tell you about how many square miles each state contains. Your job, should you accept it, is to find that chart. When and if you do, write down the following information:

    a) The largest state by population
    b) The largest state by area (square miles)
    c) The last state to enter the Union
    d) The capital city of the smallest state by population
    e) The capital city of the smallest state by area
    f) The area of Nebraska
    g) The rank order of Nebraska's statehood. In other words, was Nebraska the 25th state, the 32nd state, or whatever to enter the Union?

    When you have completed this assignment, return your completed information sheet to your teacher. You may tell your teacher that Dr. Tom Walsh says you deserve a reward!

CHAPTER ELEVEN

THE GREAT WHITE FLOOD

A True Prediction

A prediction is made when a person states that something will happen in the future. If you listen to the news or read the newspaper, you will find that people make many predictions. Some predictions, like the weather forecast, are believable. Weather forecasters rely upon science to help them make predictions. Some predictions people make have no base in science and are not so believable. Ordinary human beings have no special power to know the future.

When the native people first met white people in Nebraska, they could not predict the future. Some wise leaders among the native people did give warnings about the future. They predicted great changes would happen. One such person was Big Elk, a chief in the Omaha Tribe. In talking to his people one day, Big Elk said:

> There is a flood which will soon reach us, and I advise you to prepare for it. Soon the animals which the Great Mystery has given to us will disappear beneath this flood to return no more, and it will be hard for us. . . . I tell you this that you may be prepared for the coming change.

The flood of which Big Elk spoke began when whites moved west along the Great Platte Highway. The flood grew worse after the Kansas-Nebraska Act and with the building of the transcontinental railroad. The flood became unstoppable when Nebraska became a state. Swept away in the great white flood was the Horse and Buffalo Culture.

Reservations

In Chapter Nine, you read about the Treaty of Fort Laramie of 1851. The Government of the United States promised tribal groups areas of land to live on forever. The land promised became known as Indian reservations. You have probably heard the word reserve. The word reserve means to set something aside.

As settlers came into Nebraska they wanted to own land. They no longer wanted the native people to be able to roam and hunt freely. The Government of the United States decided to make agreements (treaties) with the native people. The government demanded that the native people give up all their claims to land. In return, the government promised to set aside an area of land for each tribe. Once on the reservations, the government wanted the native people to give up the Horse and Buffalo Culture. Children were sent to schools where they were forbidden to speak their native language. Important tribal ceremonies could not be held. Hunters were to become farmers. Some tribal groups agreed to live on reservations and peacefully accepted the offer of the government. Some tribal groups would not agree to live on reservations. Whether the native people agreed to live on reservations or not, the Government of the United States was prepared to use force to make all tribes live on reservations.

Discussion Time

The story of what happened to the native people at this time in history touches each of us. We can learn from it. Hopefully, in reading this part of Changing Nebraska, you will come to understand that there are times when people have been cruel to other people. There is nothing you can do to change what has happened in the past. There are many things you can do to make the future better for all people. The first step in building a better tomorrow is to know what has happened in the past. People can use the knowledge gained from history to judge what is being done today and to judge what is planned for tomorrow. Before you read further, spend some class discussion time talking about the kind of world you want in the future. From what you already know about Nebraska's story, what can you, as an individual, do to make a better world? A world in which all people can better understand and respect one another. A world in which people can live together in peace.

Early Flood Victims

The Horse and Buffalo Culture was something shared by each tribe in Nebraska. But, each tribe was also different. As the Government of the United States placed native people on reservations, individual agreements were signed with tribes.

The Omaha Tribe

The Omaha Tribe lived in Nebraska for many years. They lived near the Missouri River and had always been peaceful towards white people. In 1854, the Omaha Tribe signed a treaty with the Government of the United States. The Omaha agreed to give up their hunting grounds and to live on a reservation in Thurston County. Members of the Omaha Tribe live on that reservation today. You can find the Omaha Reservation by looking at a map of Nebraska. The tribal headquarters is located in the town of Macy. The reservation land lies along the Missouri River in hilly country shaped by the ancient glaciers. In 1865, the Omaha sold the northern part of their reservation to the Government of the United States. The government used that land to create a reservation for the Winnebago Tribe.

The Winnebago Tribe

The Winnebago were Woodland people who lived in the Great Lakes region of Wisconsin. As settlers moved westward into Wisconsin the Winnebago Tribe was pushed towards the west. The Government of the United States forced the Winnebago Tribe to move to the Crow Creek Reservation in South Dakota in 1863. It was a terrible place to live and many tribal members died. The Winnebago people traveled to the Omaha Reservation in the fall of 1863. In 1865, the Winnebago were given the northern part of the Omaha Reservation where they live today. You can find the Winnebago Reservation in Thurston County immediately to the north of the Omaha Reservation. The tribal headquarters is located in the town of Winnebago.

The Santee

The Santee, or Eastern Dakota, lived in Minnesota and Wisconsin. As settlers pushed into those areas, the Santee lost most of the land they had occupied and hunted. In 1862, the Santee found themselves hungry and sick. A war broke out when a few Santee tried to steal eggs from a white farmer in Minnesota. The farmer along with four other whites were killed. This incident sparked a war. The Santee people were defeated and were made to leave Minnesota. Like the Winnebago, the Santee were forced to live on the Crow Creek Reservation in South Dakota. Here where there was little to eat, many people starved. In 1866, the Santee were placed on a reservation in northeast Nebraska where they live today. You can find the Santee Reservation in Knox County.

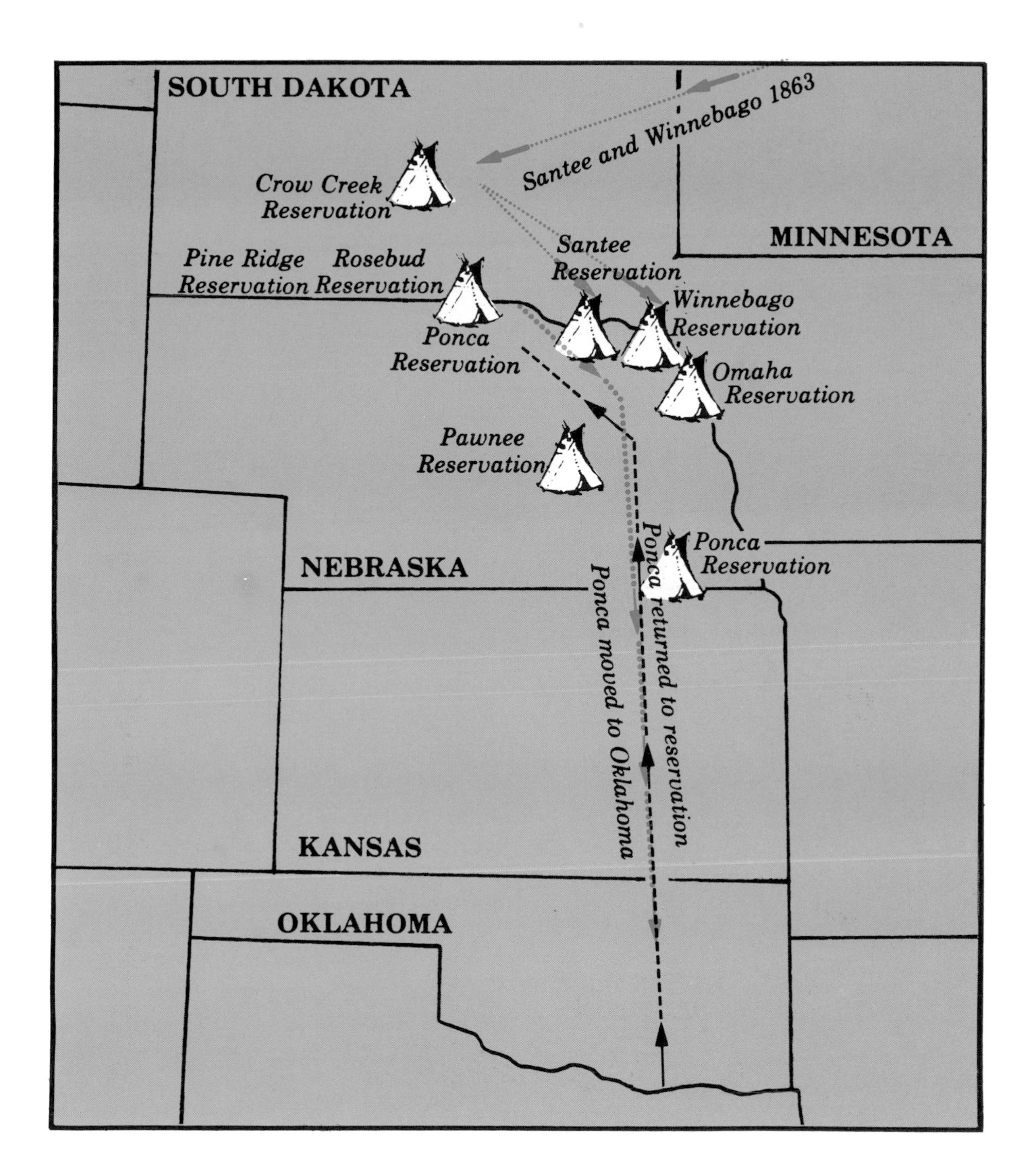

The Ponca Tribe

The Ponca, a small tribe of native people, lived in northeast Nebraska. In 1858, the Ponca Tribe signed a treaty and was promised land along the Niobrara River. In 1865, the tribe agreed to live on a smaller amount of land. The government, however, made a mistake and also promised to give the Dakota tribes the same land used by the Ponca. The Ponca were told by agents of the United States Government that they had to move to a new reservation in Oklahoma. A few of the tribal members left Nebraska and made their way to Oklahoma. In 1877, the government sent soldiers to round up the Ponca people. The soldiers forced the Ponca to move to Oklahoma.

It took over two months for the Ponca to travel to Oklahoma. The Ponca were hungry and sick and some tribal members died in making the trip. After their arrival in Oklahoma many others died. Ponca leaders asked for permission to return to Nebraska, but the government said the Ponca Tribe had to remain in Oklahoma.

Standing Bear was a Ponca chief who had asked the government not to move his people to Oklahoma. Soon after arriving in Oklahoma, Standing Bear's son knew he was about to die and begged his father to bury him in Nebraska. Disobeying government orders, Standing Bear with his family and others left Oklahoma and carried the body of Standing Bear's son back to Nebraska. When the family arrived in Nebraska, they were given shelter by the Omaha Tribe. Within a short time, Standing Bear was arrested by government soldiers. He was told he could no longer live in Nebraska and would have to return to Oklahoma.

Photograph courtesy of the Nebraska State Historical Society

Ponca Chief Standing Bear won the legal right to live in Nebraska. His fight to have Native Americans recognized as people under the law won him a place in the Nebraska Hall of Fame. A bust of Standing Bear stands in the Nebraska Hall of Fame at the State Capitol.

The story of Standing Bear quickly became news. Newspapers around the country told what happened. Many people felt that Standing Bear and the Ponca Tribe had been mistreated by the government. Two lawyers from Omaha went to court and asked that Standing Bear be set free. The court was asked to decide if Standing Bear was a person under the law.

During his trial Standing Bear moved his hand toward the judge. He asked the judge to look at his hand, and he said: "That hand is not the color of your hand, but if I pierce it I shall feel pain. The blood that will flow from mine will be the same color as yours. I am a man." The court decided that Standing Bear was a person under the law and that the government could not force him to live on a reservation against his will.

After the trial, Standing Bear was granted a piece of land near his home along the Niobrara. Over 100 of his fellow tribe members joined him in living in Nebraska. Standing Bear lived to be an old man and died in his beloved Nebraska in 1908. Although there are Ponca people living in Nebraska today, the tribal land was sold and the Ponca Tribe of Nebraska no longer exists.

Photograph courtesy of the Nebraska State Historical Society

Pawnee School at Genoa.

The Pawnee

The Pawnee at one time were the largest tribal group in Nebraska. Diseases brought by white people killed many tribal members. The Pawnee were also bitter enemies of the Dakota tribes and had suffered great losses in warfare. In 1833, the Pawnee gave up all claims to land south of the Platte River. They were to move their villages to the Loup River area and the government promised to protect them from the Western Dakota and to make available schooling and assistance. In 1857, the Pawnee made another agreement with the government. They gave up all land in Nebraska except for a small reservation along the Loup River in Nance County. The government opened a school for Pawnee youngsters at Genoa and again promised to protect the Pawnee from their enemies.

Things continued to grow worse for the Pawnee. White settlers wanted to obtain their reservation land. With the coming of railroads, the buffalo were killed off and the Pawnee had fewer resources. The Dakota tribes continued to raid Pawnee villages and the Pawnee were given little protection by the government. In the summer of 1873, a Pawnee hunting party had found a nice herd of buffalo near Trenton. There were about 300 Pawnee men, women, and children in the hunting party. Soon a group of 100 Western Dakota hunters came upon the scene. A fight broke out and within a short period of time another 800 Dakota hunters showed up. The Dakota rained arrows and bullets down upon the Pawnee who were trapped in a deep ravine. Many Pawnee men, women, and children were killed in the fight. A monument has been put up by the Nebraska State Historical Society honoring the Pawnee who died at "Massacre Canyon." You can find that place by looking at a map of Nebraska and finding Hitchcock County.

After the massacre in Hitchcock County, Pawnee tribal leaders decided it was best to leave Nebraska. Since there were many settlers who wanted the Pawnee land, the Government of the United States quickly agreed to give the Pawnee new reservation land in Oklahoma. By the end of 1875, the Pawnee had left Nebraska.

A Trail of Tears

Not all native people peacefully accepted reservation life. The Ponca, the Omaha, the Pawnee, the Winnebago, and the Santee had been greatly weakened by disease, starvation, and warfare over a period of years. They were cruelly treated at times, and they had little choice but to accept the great changes that were predicted by wise leaders like Big Elk. Other tribal groups took to the warpath to preserve the Horse and Buffalo Culture. You will read about their final days in the next chapter.

Important Ideas to Remember from the Great White Flood

Long before white settlers came to Nebraska, some tribal wise men had predicted that white people would come and destroy the Horse and Buffalo Culture.

The Government of the United States wanted the native people to give up all claims to land in Nebraska. In return, the government moved tribal groups to reservations.

The Government of the United States wanted native people to live on reservations and to learn the ways of white people. The government wanted to destroy the Horse and Buffalo Culture.

Members of the Omaha, Winnebago, and Santee tribes live on reservation land in northeast Nebraska today.

The Ponca Tribe of Nebraska no longer exists today, but Chief Standing Bear, a famous Ponca leader, was elected to the Nebraska Hall of Fame.

The Pawnee Tribe gave up their reservation land in Nebraska and moved to Oklahoma in 1875.

Things to Do

1. Many Native American people make their home in Nebraska today. They are very proud of their history and you can discover more about Nebraska's native people by using the guide words listed below.

   BIG ELK
   STANDING BEAR
   OMAHA TRIBE
   WINNEBAGO TRIBE
   SANTEE TRIBE
   PONCA TRIBE
   PAWNEE TRIBES

2. Tribal groups in Nebraska hold annual gatherings called pow-wows. These gatherings are often open to the general public. Usually you can share in dancing, music, and food. If you are interested in attending a pow-wow on one of the Nebraska reservations, write to the tribal council for information.

CHAPTER TWELVE
THE FINAL DAYS

Hopelessly Lost

I call to the four winds
I cannot find me.
I seek the great buffalo herds
I cannot find me.
I dance to the beat of the drum
I cannot find me.
Do my senses lie?
I cannot find me.
Oh Great Father, I cannot find me.

There are times in life when change can be powerful. You have probably read or heard about great disasters that bring sudden change. A flood, for example, strikes a community and destroys many homes. Those people who see their homes destroyed in such a disaster suffer greatly. Sometimes it is hard for those who suffer from such tragedies to recover. In a sense, what was destroyed was a part of them.

So it was for the native people of the Horse and Buffalo Culture. The great nomadic hunters, in particular, valued a way of life that demanded freedom, huge buffalo herds, and large amounts of territory. As settlers entered Nebraska, they wanted to own land. They killed off the buffalo herds. They no longer wanted the native people to roam freely. Two different cultures with two different ways of life led to a painful conflict. One culture was more powerful than the other, and when the conflict was over the native people found their lives changed forever. The change forced upon the native people was so strong, they seemed hopelessly lost in their own land.

Drawing the Lines

According to the Treaty of Fort Laramie of 1851, travelers heading west along the Oregon and Mormon Trails were to be allowed to travel in peace. The tribal groups most involved with that agreement were the Western Dakota, the Cheyenne, and the Arapaho. The Western Dakota were divided into several tribal groups, and included amongst those tribes were the Oglala and Brule. The Cheyenne were divided into two major tribal groups, the Northern and Southern Cheyenne. All of these tribal groups allied themselves as a single force to resist the efforts made to take their land, to kill off the buffalo herds, and to place them on reservations.

About three years after the Treaty of Fort Laramie was signed, events happened which saw the two sides draw the lines. The first incident occurred in August, 1854. Thousands of native people had gathered near Fort Laramie to receive the goods promised them by the treaty. A Mormon party was heading towards Utah along the Great Platte Highway when a lame cow wandered into a Dakota camp. The cow was killed, and the hide was stripped from the carcass. The owner of the cow stopped at Fort Laramie and complained. He demanded to be paid for the cow. The army commander sent a young lieutenant by the name of John L. Grattan to the Dakota camp to arrest the person who killed the cow.

Sending Grattan was a poor choice. Grattan had just graduated from the military academy in West Point, New York. He was anxious to fight Indians. At one time he had boasted that all Indians were cowards and that with 30 men he could defeat all the Indians on the Great Plains.

If it was a mistake to send Grattan, ignorance made the mistake worse. According to Dakota customs, it would have been disgraceful for a warrior to surrender and be taken prisoner. A Brule chief named Conquering Bear explained to Lieutenant Grattan that payment for the cow would be made at Fort Laramie. The young lieutenant insisted that the guilty person be turned over to him. When Conquering Bear refused his demands, Lieutenant Grattan returned to his troops who had taken positions in the camp.

Lieutenant Grattan had a detachment of 30 men along with a cannon. Without warning he ordered his men to open fire. Conquering Bear was killed by the army shelling and shooting. The warriors within the camp immediately attacked Grattan and his men. All of the soldiers were killed in the brief fight. Many warriors were ready to attack Fort Laramie and drive the army out, but they were calmed by their chiefs who led their people away from the area.

The Grattan incident was called a massacre by newspapers across the country. The native people were blamed for what had happened and the United States Army was called upon to teach the Indians a lesson. The army had no way to launch a strike against the native people. The railroad had not yet been built through the Platte Valley, and there was no way to move large numbers of soldiers.

In the summer of 1855, the army ordered General William S. Harney to lead about 600 men from Fort Leavenworth, Kansas, into the Platte Valley. Harney and his men had one purpose. They were to hunt down and defeat any group of nomadics they could find. By early September, Harney and his men had traveled up the Platte Valley and were near Ash Hollow in Garden County. At the Blue Water Creek they overtook a band of Brule led by Chief Little Thunder. The chief met with General Harney and was told that he was to surrender any warriors involved with the murder of Lieutenant Grattan. Before Chief Little Thunder could return to his camp, General Harney ordered his men to attack. The soldiers killed 86 Brule in that attack and took the rest of the band prisoners. Harney ordered the prisoners put in chains and shamelessly marched them to Fort Laramie. With bitterness in their hearts, the Brule named General Harney the "Squaw Killer." (See map, Blue Water Creek incident, September, 1855.)

Upon his arrival at Fort Laramie, General Harney ordered that the Indian agent not deliver supplies to the native people. Through the Treaty of Fort Laramie of 1851, the government had promised to give the tribal groups involved up to $50,000 in goods each year. Harney was going to make the native people accept peace or be punished. The native people felt they could no longer trust the government. Native leaders were angry over how their people had been treated. Although General Harney did succeed in bringing a brief period of peace, the lines were drawn and war seemed likely.

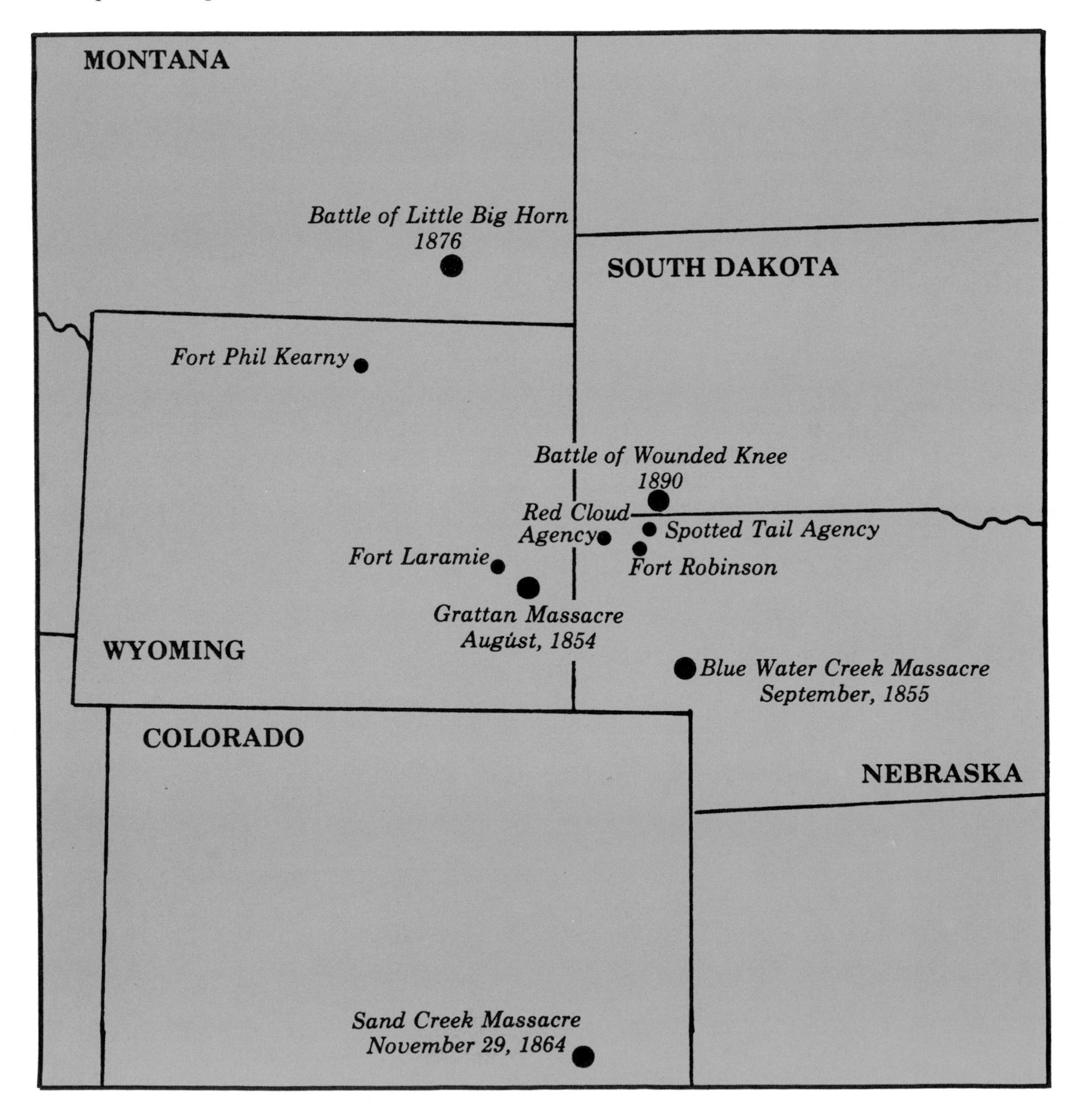

The Broken Peace

In 1858, gold was discovered in Colorado and once again gold seekers pushed westward along the Great Platte Highway. The native people were angry about the new flood of whites heading west. With the outbreak of the Civil War in 1860, army troops were used to fight the Confederacy. Now the Dakota, Cheyenne, and Arapaho began to strike back. Mounted warriors used raid warfare to spread fear all along the Platte Valley. The Nebraska, Colorado, and Kansas frontier was in a state of panic. Both native tribesmen and white settlers were guilty of acts of cruelty. One of the most terrible acts of cruelty happened in 1864 in eastern Colorado.

A Southern Cheyenne chief named Black Kettle had urged his people to remain peaceful during all the fighting. Black Kettle was told by the government that he and his people could safely camp on the Sand Creek Reservation near Fort Lyons in eastern Colorado. Black Kettle was joined by a small group of Arapaho under Chief Left Hand. All together there were about 700 people in the camp, of which 500 were women and children. At dawn on November 29, 1864, Colonel John Chivington led a group of Colorado volunteers on an attack against the helpless Cheyenne and Arapaho. The attack lasted several hours and many Cheyenne and Arapaho were killed. Most of the dead were women and children. Black Kettle survived the attack, but Chief Left Hand was killed. Black Kettle led his people away from Sand Creek while Colonel Chivington's men took scalps from their victims. When word of the Sand Creek Massacre spread, native leaders in the area smoked the pipe of war. They pledged to fight the whites forever. (See map, Sand Creek Massacre, November, 1864.)

From War to Reservations

When the Civil War ended in 1865, settlers came to Nebraska and surrounding states to obtain land. The transcontinental railroad was built across Nebraska. The railroad not only brought new settlers, but the buffalo herds were slaughtered. It is estimated that in 1850, before the Kansas-Nebraska Act, over 50,000,000 buffalo lived on the Great Plains. By 1885, only a few hundred buffalo roamed the plains. The resource needed for the Horse and Buffalo Culture was gone.

The discovery of gold in Montana and South Dakota also spelled trouble for the people of the Horse and Buffalo Culture. During the Civil War gold had been discovered in Montana. Once again gold seekers made their way into territory that had been promised to the native people by the Treaty of Fort Laramie. The government intended to build a road north from Fort Laramie into Montana and open forts along the road to protect the gold seekers. As had been done in 1851, the government called for a peace meeting at Fort Laramie. Government officials demanded that native leaders sign a treaty allowing the government to open the "Bozemen Trail" into Montana. Western Dakota chiefs refused to sign such an agreement. The army pushed ahead anyway, and built a fort called Fort Phil Kearny. This led to constant warfare between soldiers and the Cheyenne and the Dakota.

In an effort to end the fighting, the government called for another peace meeting at Fort Laramie in 1868. Again, a treaty was offered to the native people. The government agreed to close the Bozeman Trail and to leave Fort Phil Kearny. The Oglala Chief Red Cloud and the Brule Chief Spotted Tail agreed to accept the creation of a large reservation in South Dakota known as the Great Sioux Reservation. In accepting reservation life, the Dakota were promised they could hunt buffalo in the North Platte and Republican River Valleys for as long as the buffalo roamed. Although they gave up their claims to land in Nebraska, the Dakota and Cheyenne remained in control of the Black Hills of South Dakota and the Powder River Country of Wyoming and Montana.

Photograph courtesy of the Nebraska State Historical Society

Chief Red Cloud, respected Oglala Chief, fought against the army along the Bozeman Trail and forced the government to abandon Fort Phil Kearny.

Photograph courtesy of the Nebraska State Historical Society

Chief Spotted Tail, respected Brule Chief, allied himself with Red Cloud in an effort to protect Dakota homeland.

In preparing for reservation life, Red Cloud and Spotted Tail agreed to bring their people to government agencies in northwest Nebraska. The Red Cloud Agency was eventually located along the White River near Crawford. The Spotted Tail Agency was located along the White River about fifty miles east of Crawford. The government promised to provide food to the native people at the agencies. In 1874, the government established Fort Robinson near the Red Cloud Agency. Here the government stationed soldiers to make certain the Oglala and Brule remained peaceful. (See map on page 100, Red Cloud Agency and Spotted Tail Agency.)

Not all native leaders accepted the Treaty of Fort Laramie of 1868. Dakota chiefs Sitting Bull and Crazy Horse refused to accept reservation life. They continued to hunt and live as they had always known life in the Horse and Buffalo Culture. In 1874, gold was discovered in the Black Hills of South Dakota. This was land sacred to the Dakota tribes. It was land promised to the native people under the Treaties of Fort Laramie. Gold seekers poured into the Black Hills and another agreement was broken. The Government of the United States asked Red Cloud and Spotted Tail to agree to sell the Black Hills. The two chiefs agreed to give up tribal hunting rights in Nebraska, but they refused to sell the Black Hills. Angered by this stand, the government issued an order in December, 1875. The government ordered all members of Dakota tribes to report to the Indian agencies by January 31, 1876. Those persons not on agency land by that date would be considered at war with the United States.

Sitting Bull and Crazy Horse refused to obey the government order. They led large bands of Dakota who had been joined by Northern Cheyenne and Arapaho. In March, 1876, the government sent troops into Wyoming, South Dakota, and Montana looking to defeat the native people in battle. There were several small fights in which the Dakota and Cheyenne skillfully defeated the soldiers. Finally, the native people set up a large camp on the Little Big Horn River in Montana.

In mid June, Chief Sitting Bull had a vision that he would do well in a great battle against the soldiers. His chance came on June 25, 1876, when a force under General George A. Custer attacked the camp of native people. Warriors led by Sitting Bull and Crazy Horse surrounded General Custer and killed the general along with over 200 cavalrymen in one hour of fighting. Custer's defeat shocked the nation. People demanded that the government force the native people to live on reservations forever. (See map on page 100, Custer's defeat, June, 1876.)

Following the Battle of the Little Big Horn, the government demanded that the Western Dakota tribes give up their claim to the Black Hills. This was agreed to in a treaty signed by Red Cloud and Spotted Tail in September, 1876. They also agreed to move to the Great Sioux Reservation in South Dakota. Fearful that Red Cloud might lead his people into war, government soldiers invaded Red Cloud's camp near Chadron in October, 1876, and took from his people all their horses and weapons.

In the spring of 1877, Crazy Horse and 2,000 of his followers surrendered to government soldiers at the Red Cloud Agency in Nebraska. Later that year, the government arrested Crazy Horse and took him to Fort Robinson. Crazy Horse died at Fort Robinson after he was bayonetted by a soldier. The Oglala and Brule were made to leave Nebraska in October, 1877. The Oglala were placed on the Pine Ridge Reservation in South Dakota while the Brule were forced to live on the Rosebud Reservation. (See map on page 93 to identify the Pine Ridge and Rosebud Reservations.)

Sitting Bull fled to Canada after the Battle of the Little Big Horn. He returned to the United States in 1881 and surrendered to government soldiers. He was moved to the Standing Rock Reservation in South Dakota in 1883. In December, 1890, government agents tried to arrest Sitting Bull. They suspected he was trying to lead his people into war. Sitting Bull refused to be arrested and was killed by Indian police. The incident led to panic. White settlers thought the Dakota tribes were going to war again. The army was called in, and finally at Wounded Knee, South Dakota, near Fort Robinson, an attempt was made to disarm a group of native people. Shooting broke out and over 150 native people and 25 soldiers were killed. This terrible event marked the end of the Indian Wars. (See map on page 100, Battle of Wounded Knee, December, 1890.)

Photograph courtesy of the Nebraska State Historical Society

Western Dakota Chief Sitting Bull helped lead the last campaigns against the army in an attempt to preserve the Horse and Buffalo Culture.

End of an Era

The word era refers to a period of time in history. In Nebraska's history, the Horse and Buffalo Culture was an important era. It was a period of time when the native people lived a lifestyle that depended upon the gifts of nature. The nomadic tribes, in particular, fought to keep the free way of life they valued. You know by now that nothing stays the same. The Western Dakota tribes were placed on reservations in South Dakota. The Northern Cheyenne eventually were placed on a reservation in Montana. The Arapaho went to the Wind River Reservation in Wyoming. The Government of the United States expected the native people to adopt the ways of the white culture. This was not easy. "We are strangers in the land where we were born," said one Omaha leader. The pain of adjusting to great and sudden change—"Oh Great Father, I cannot find me."

Important Ideas to Remember from the Final Days

It is difficult and sometimes painful for people to adjust to sudden and far reaching change that may affect their lives.

The great nomadic tribes of western Nebraska fought to keep the Horse and Buffalo Culture from being destroyed.

The Grattan incident of 1854 set off a terrible war between the Western Dakota, Cheyenne, and Arapaho Tribes and the Government of the United States.

During the Indian Wars acts of cruelty were committed by people involved with the wars.

As the Indian Wars continued, the native people found themselves in a terrible position: more settlers came to Nebraska and the surrounding area; the buffalo herds were slaughtered; agreements with the government were broken with regularity; and the United States Army was used to make almost continuous war with the nomadic tribes.

The discovery of gold in Colorado, Montana, and South Dakota led to much trouble between the nomadic tribes and the Government of the United States.

The defeat of General Custer at the Little Big Horn spelled the end for the Horse and Buffalo Culture. Great pressure was put on the government to force the nomadic tribes on to reservations.

Life on the reservations was painful for the native people because they were expected to give up a culture they had developed over many years.

Things to Do

1. Learn more about the final days of the Horse and Buffalo Culture by following these guide words to the library.

   OGLALA TRIBE
   BRULE TRIBE
   HUNKPAPA TRIBE
   MINNECONJOU TRIBE

CHEYENNE TRIBE
ARAPAHO TRIBE
RED CLOUD
SPOTTED TAIL
LITTLE THUNDER
BLACK KETTLE
SITTING BULL
CRAZY HORSE
FORT LARAMIE
FORT PHIL KEARNY
FORT ROBINSON
FORT MCPHERSON
FORT NIOBRARA
FORT HARTSUFF
GENERAL WILLIAM HARNEY
GENERAL GEORGE CUSTER
COLONEL JOHN CHIVINGTON
TREATY OF FORT LARAMIE OF 1868
RED CLOUD AGENCY
SPOTTED TAIL AGENCY
PINE RIDGE RESERVATION
ROSEBUD RESERVATION
BATTLE OF THE LITTLE BIG HORN
WOUNDED KNEE

2. Pretend you are a reporter who works for a big New York newspaper. The time is shortly after the Civil War. You have been sent by your editor to the Platte Valley to do a story about the fighting that is going on with the nomadic tribes. You interview local settlers, soldiers and army officers, and the leaders and members of nomadic tribes. Now you must write a story for your newspaper. The topic of your story is the Indian Wars. You must give an objective account of how the wars started, how people from all sides feel about the wars, and what you think might be done to end the wars. In writing this story you may consult any resources you can find. Maps might be helpful to your readers in understanding where events have taken place.

   P.S.—This could become a class project by having a team of reporters cover the story. Each reporter or small group of reporters could be given specific assignments. For example, some might interview Chief Red Cloud while others interview General Harney. Some might interview a worker on the Union Pacific Railroad while others interview an Oglala hunter and warrior.

CHAPTER THIRTEEN

THE DREAM CHASERS—PART I

Sharing Dreams

There are lots of things human beings share in common. One thing we all seem to share is the ability to dream. Dreaming is not limited to the times when you sleep. People dream all the time! Do you ever think about the future and what life will be like for you? That is a form of dreaming. You imagine yourself at some other place in another time. You can see things in your own mind. You might even share your dreams with a good friend, a person you trust.

Personal note from the author—I'll share a secret with you. I have always been a dreamer. When I was your age, I frequently dreamed about what I might do as an adult. Sometimes I saw myself as a farmer or a rancher. Sometimes I was a great athlete. I even dreamed of being an astronaut long before there was a space program. There were times when I shared my dreams with friends who had similar dreams. One of my friends also dreamed about going into space, and we would pretend to be astronauts making great voyages to faraway planets.

When I got to be an adult, my dreaming did not stop. I still dream about things I may or may not be able to do some day. One thing I have discovered about dreaming is that some dreams become very important. It is the important dreams that I chase. I have caught a few and they have become real. Sometimes I am disappointed, but more often I find catching dreams to be the most important part of life.

Dreaming dreams is shaping life.
Dreaming dreams, that's no waste.
Pity those who never dream.
They never see what might have been.

The Dream Chasers

Chasing dreams brought people to Nebraska after the Civil War. Imagine yourself living in an eastern city in the United States. You work as a laborer for less than a dollar per day. You hear about free land available in Nebraska through the Homestead Act. Would you be tempted to move and chase the dream of a better life in Nebraska?

Think of yourself as living in Europe. You are a poor farmer with little land. You owe heavy taxes to the government and are in great debt. One day a friend comes to your house. The friend is carrying a piece of paper and seems excited. You read the piece of paper which is printed by the Union Pacific Railroad Company. The paper tells you that the Union Pacific owns millions of acres of land in Nebraska, a place located in the central part of the

United States. The Union Pacific promises to sell the land cheaply to settlers. People can take up to ten years to pay for the land they buy. Not only is the land cheap and the terms reasonable, but Nebraska sounds like heaven. The piece of paper says that Nebraska is a beautiful place with rich land. Nebraska winters are mild and the climate is healthful, according to the paper you read. Your friend tells you that many of your neighbors are going to pack up and move to Nebraska where they can buy big farms, escape heavy taxes, and lead a better life. "Come on," your friend says, "we can all live together in our own community. Your children will be free of heavy debt when they grow up." Would you be tempted to leave your homeland and chase the dream of a new life that could bring great riches and happiness?

What if you were a black person living in Tennessee? You had been a slave and had worked on a large plantation. Even after slavery was ended, life was difficult for black people because of prejudice. During the Civil War it was often impossible to obtain food and many people went hungry. When the war ended you were no longer a slave, but other bad things happened. Angry whites took their anger out on you and other black people. You were afraid for yourself and your family. One day you hear that a group of blacks is moving to a place called Nebraska. You hear there are jobs in Nebraska, and there is land available for farming. You can join your friends and move to Nebraska, or you can remain in Tennessee and live in fear and certain poverty. What would you do? Would you take a chance and chase the dream of a new life?

The people who came to Nebraska during this period of the late 1860's through the early 1900's were dream chasers. They had many reasons for coming, but they all believed life was going to be better because they came to Nebraska. For some who came, their dreams were fulfilled. For others who came, their dreams were shattered. Nebraska, that place located in the center of the United States, made great changes in the lives of the people who came to occupy it. So too, did the new wave of people who came to the state bring change to Nebraska.

The Dream Chasers Meet Reality

After the Civil War, people began coming to Nebraska in greater numbers. Some were brought by steamboats up the Missouri River. Others traveled by railroad across Iowa and then came across the Missouri River to enter Nebraska. When the Union Pacific and Burlington Railroads were built, the railroad companies sent agents out across the United States and western Europe encouraging people to come to Nebraska. Many people came to Nebraska by covered wagon. These were people who lived in the East. They packed what they could in a wagon and set out for Nebraska.

Home on the Farm

The river towns along the Missouri River were jumping-off places for those settlers who came to farm. Here a settler could find a government land office, file a claim on a piece of land, and then move to the newly claimed farm. The earliest settlers took timberland along streams and creeks where they could find trees to build cabins and fences. As the population spread westward, there were fewer trees. The only building material available was sod. As the native village dwellers had done for years in building earth lodges, the new settlers made their homes from the good earth.

Building a cabin or a sod house took time. When the dream chasers first arrived they had to think about a place to live, food to eat, and water to drink. Since they had come great distances, they usually traveled with only the basic necessities. Settlers would arrive at their new farm site with a few clothes, a little food, some basic tools, a few dishes and utensils, some personal treasures like a family Bible or special heirlooms (HEIR-LOOMS), and maybe a cow, pigs, or chickens. If they were lucky enough to locate near a stream, water was readily available. If not, they had to locate the nearest water source and haul water to their farm site.

For a period of time after arriving, settlers lived in temporary shelters. If they arrived in a wagon, the wagon would likely be their home for awhile. A settler might dig a hole into the side of a hill to make a dwelling. By digging into the earth six or seven feet and enclosing the entry way, dream chasers created underground houses, called dugouts, that were satisfactory until they could build a permanent shelter above ground.

Sod houses were built by using a plow to break the tough prairie sod. The native grasses on the prairie were thick and had long roots. Breaking the sod was no easy matter. After plowing several long straight strips, the sod was cut into three-foot pieces called sod bricks. A sod house was built by laying the sod bricks on top of one another. If you look at a brick wall, you will see that the layers of brick are staggered and that cement is used to fill in between the cracks. A sod house builder did much the same thing. The builder staggered the sod bricks and filled in the cracks with dirt.

In making a sod house roof, the builder would use coarse prairie hay, poles, and crooked tree branches to hold up layers of sod and dirt. As you can imagine, when it rained the roof frequently leaked. Mud and water would fall down from the ceiling. Some sod dwellers would nail a bedsheet or a piece of cloth to the ceiling to catch the dirt that fell from above.

Sod houses, or "soddies" as they were called, were like earth lodges in that they were warm in the winter and cool in the summer. Of course, there were problems with living in a sod house. The sod was usually infested with fleas. During the warmer months, it was impossible to keep fleas from getting into your clothing and bedding. The early settlers also told stories about snakes burrowing into the sod walls and roofs. Living in a sod house, with all its problems, was better than living in a dugout or a wagon.

Photograph courtesy of the Nebraska State Historical Society

Farm life on the Nebraska frontier was far from glamorous.

The dream chasers found that farm life in Nebraska was difficult at best. With limited surface water, people dug into the earth to find ground water. In some locations wells were 20 to 30 feet deep. In other places, water was found 100 feet or more below the surface. Wells were dug by hand, and many a well digger met death when trapped in a deep well as the walls caved in.

Pioneer farmers rarely went hungry. Corn was the major crop. Planted by opening the prairie sod and inserting seed, corn grew as well for the newcomers as it had for the native people. There was also an abundance of rabbit, prairie chicken, deer, and some buffalo. Gardens were usually planted in the spring and provided many delicious vegetables during the growing season.

Pioneer farm families found the climate of Nebraska to be less beautiful than the land promoters had claimed. Just as we know today, Nebraska's winters can be mild or they can be bitter cold with terrible blizzards. Nebraska summers ranged between mild and wet to hot and dry. One thing the dream chasers were not prepared for was the terrible grasshopper invasions that began in the late 1850's. Eight times between 1857 and 1875, Nebraska was invaded by Rocky Mountain Grasshoppers. They came by the millions from the west. Probably the worst grasshopper invasion occurred in July, 1874. It had been dry, and Nebraska farmers were struggling to raise sufficient crops for survival. Then, in late July, the sky was darkened with grasshoppers, so many grasshoppers that their wings made the sound of an approaching storm. Corn fields were devoured. Fruit trees were stripped. They even ate holes in cloth and the rugs used to cover garden and flower patches. Little food was left for the winter. This was reality in Nebraska. For some, dreams had turned to nightmares. They could no longer withstand drought, back-breaking labor, prairie fires, insects, loneliness, and the general discomfort of frontier life. Some wagons headed back east in the mid-1870's carrying the message of shattered dreams.

Are Tough Times Good Times?

Farm life on the Nebraska frontier was harsh. Many people gave up. They found pursuing their dreams demanded a high price. Those who stayed turned to family and friends to soften the blows of reality.

There is a story about the Hawthorne family who farmed in the central Platte Valley during the mid-1870's. Their crops were destroyed by grasshoppers. Their friends and neighbors suffered the same fate. People throughout the area were leaving their farms to seek other employment. A group called the Nebraska Relief and Aid Society was organized to collect money, clothing, and other donations to help the poor farm families of Nebraska. Boxes of goods from around the country were sent to Nebraska.

One day the Hawthornes and many of their neighbors gathered to open some boxes of clothing they had received from New York. In opening the boxes the dream chasers found no clothing for children, one suit of clothes for a man, and many fancy clothes for women that could never be worn for doing the heavy farm labor required on a frontier farm. As Mrs. Hawthorne examined the clothing, it seemed as if this was the last straw. She put her head down on a table and cried.

Making the best of a tragic situation, a male neighbor of Mrs. Hawthorne's quickly picked up a fancy woman's hat that contained many big feathers. He turned to Mrs. Hawthorne with a silly grin and told her he was wearing his new plowing hat. Everybody began to laugh, and soon all the men, women, and children put on all the fancy dresses and clothing and began to dance. There were no refreshments served at the house, but the people who left the Hawthorne house that night had been refreshed.

Discussion Time

This is a good time for you to talk to your family and community residents about the dream chasers who came to farm in Nebraska during this time. Share with your family or friends the story of the Hawthorne family. Here are some ideas you may want to talk about. You can agree or disagree with the ideas, but it is important to share, to talk, and to think.

Idea #1—Friends and family can give a person strength at times when it seems most needed.

Idea #2—Material wealth may not be the secret to human happiness.

Idea #3—Sometimes, what appear to be the hardest moments in life turn out to be the best moments.

Change Marches On

The dream chasers who came to farm brought great change to Nebraska. The wide-open spaces began to be carved up into individual pieces. Windmills to acquire water started to dot the land. People brought different languages, customs, and beliefs to Nebraska. Frontier schools were established where young people were taught the three R's of "reading, riting, and rithmetic." As farmers became better established they began to raise crops to sell for cash. The growth of towns and railroads made it possible for farmers to sell surplus (SUR-PLUS) products like grain, dairy products, and animals. Farming was becoming a business. In business, people sell a product to make a profit. How different this was from the days when the native people grew crops as basic food resources. How different this was from the days when the earliest pioneer farmers staked out a land claim and grew enough food to survive. Farm life was beginning to change, but it was the dream chasers who made modern farm life possible.

Compare this picture to that of the sod house farm on page 112. What differences and similarities do you see? What made those differences possible?

Important Ideas to Remember from the Dream Chasers—Part I

One form of dreaming is people projecting themselves into different places and times. People who do this type of dreaming often see new possibilities for themselves.

Some people are pleased by what they see as new possibilities in their dreams.

Dreams offering new possibilities can become so appealing that some people try to make their dreams come true. These individuals can be called dream chasers.

Following the Civil War, many dream chasers moved to Nebraska to make a new life.

One group of dream chasers who came to Nebraska were people who came to occupy the land as farmers.

The farm dream chasers came to Nebraska for many reasons. They were attracted by available land, the freedom to lead a better life, the promise of a better future for their children, and some came because of the exaggerated claims made by land promoters.

The farm dream chasers came to Nebraska by railroad, by wagon, by river boat, and even on foot.

After claiming their land, the dream chasers were faced with the difficult task of starting life on the prairie.

Farm houses in early Nebraska were cabins built of logs in the wooded areas along streams and rivers. In places where wood was unavailable, pioneer farmers made their houses out of sod.

Farm life during this time was difficult. All labor was done by hand. Life was sometimes lonely with neighbors living at great distances. Water was not easily available for all farmers, and wells had to be hand dug to great depths into the earth.

Prairie fires sometimes raged out of control and posed great danger to frontier farmers. Since farm families were so isolated, the weather could be dangerous. Sudden storms caught people unprepared which sometimes resulted in injuries and death.

Insects, particularly grasshoppers, posed a great threat to crops. The invasion of destructive grasshoppers caused many people to give up farming on the Nebraska frontier.

The farm dream chasers who stuck it out on the Nebraska frontier often depended on family and friends to give them strength during difficult times.

Modern farm life was made possible by the efforts of the early farm dream chasers.

Things to Do

1. Farming is an important way of life and business in Nebraska today. Learn more about the early history of Nebraska farming by checking out this list of guide words.

   HOMESTEAD ACT
   TIMBER CULTURE ACT
   PRE-EMPTION ACT
   KINKAID ACT
   IMMIGRANT HOUSE
   NEBRASKA STATE BOARD OF IMMIGRATION
   SOD BUSTERS
   SOD HOUSES
   WINDMILLS

2. Challenge and note from the author. On occasion you will see poetic statements in this book. I write those statements because I want to express my feelings about a subject. Here is a challenge for you. Frontier farm life is a subject full of emotion and feeling. It took courage and determination to farm on the Nebraska frontier. Imagine a character living on the frontier in the 1870's or 1880's. This person is a woman. She is the mother of four young children. She can be any nationality or race. Two of her children were born in a Nebraska sod house where no doctor was present. The nearest neighbor lives over ten miles away, so she rarely gets to see another person let alone another woman. Her skin has become dry and tough due to her exposure to the sun and the wind. She works hard in the fields and doing the household chores. On occasion her husband leaves her alone on the farm with the children so that he can find employment in the nearest town to earn money for the family. This woman has not seen members of her own family for years. How does she feel? If she could speak and express herself to you, what would she say? Write her statement in a poetic fashion. Don't worry about style, measure, or verse. Just let her speak.
3. Invite a speaker to your classroom. Every county has an extension agent. Extension agents are people who work with farmers and help farm families. Explain to your local extension agent that you have been studying about frontier farm life in Nebraska. Ask your extension agent to tell your class about modern farming. What are some of the greatest challenges facing the modern farmer? How about farm families? How has life changed for them in recent years?

CHAPTER FOURTEEN
THE DREAM CHASERS—PART II

Room For Lots of Dreamers

Dreamers come in all shapes and sizes. There are male dreamers and female dreamers. Dreamers are made up of all races, creeds, and colors. The truth is, dreamers are people and not just one kind of people. All kinds of people came to Nebraska after the Civil War. There were many people who came to Nebraska with no intention of farming. These were people with other dreams. Nebraska was a changing place at this time, a place where dreamers considered all sorts of possibilities.

Planners and Dreamers

A planner is a person who puts together a plan to realize a dream. Before building a house, people will draw a plan for the house. The plan lays out in detail what is to be done in order to build the house correctly.

Some dream chasers who came to Nebraska during this time were planners. They came with plans in mind to achieve their dreams. Towns and cities were usually started by planners. In some cases the planners believed there was an opportunity to make money. They would acquire land and then

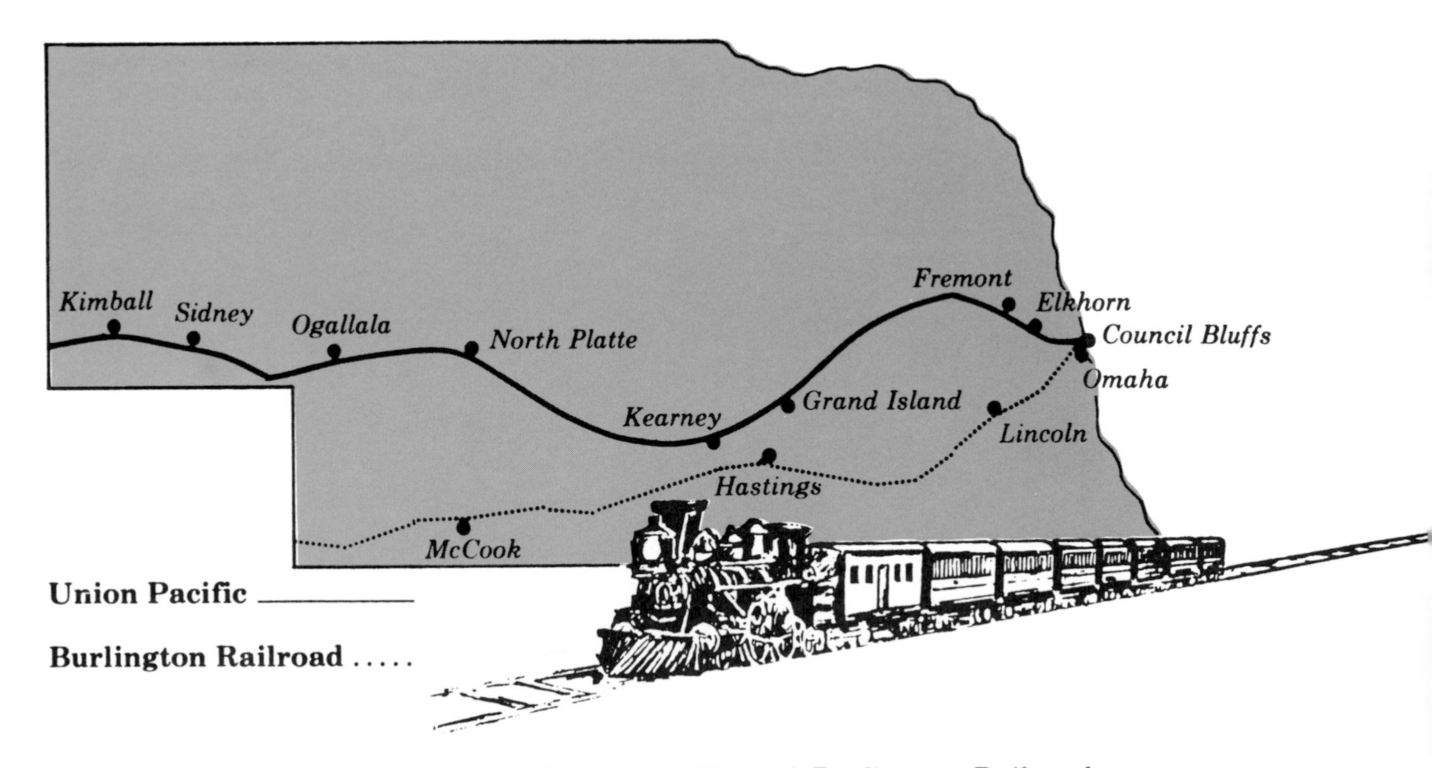

This map shows the routes of the Union Pacific and Burlington Railroads across Nebraska. Why did so many towns along the railroad routes grow and prosper? Why did so many towns along the Missouri River grow and prosper?

sell lots or small pieces of their land. If the planners were successful in starting a town, they could make big profits by selling off land in small pieces. As people moved into a town they bought lots to build houses and buildings. When the railroads were built across Nebraska, towns often succeeded or failed depending on the routes selected by the railroads.

Transportation and People

The means of transportation and transportation routes had much to do with the success and/or failure of towns established in early Nebraska. Do you think there are towns in Nebraska today which grow or decline because of transportation means and routes? What could you do to find information to answer that question?

There were a number of planners with religious beliefs who came to Nebraska during this time. These people often established communities for people to live and share their beliefs. Ethnic communities were commonly established in Nebraska. People of a particular nationality or race were invited to come and make a new life in Nebraska. Wilber in Saline County was founded as a Czech community. O'Neill in Holt County was an Irish settlement. Grand Island in Hall County was planned by a group of German settlers. Grant City in Franklin County was planned by a group of black homesteaders who had migrated from the South.

Towns established in Nebraska at this time usually followed a pattern in their development. Streets were laid out and were often named after important people like presidents or generals. If the town was a railroad town, the main street often ran parallel to the railroad tracks. The first businesses established in the early towns were outfitting stores to supply the local settlers with goods and seed. A blacksmith shop and a livery stable were also important businesses because of the dependence upon the horse. A lumber yard was needed to supply lumber and building materials if the town was to grow and prosper. A hotel was essential for visitors and newcomers who needed temporary shelter. Newspapers were organized early in towns. A newspaper not only provided news, but it was a great way for the town founders to advertise their town.

Photograph courtesy of the Nebraska State Historical Society

Main street looked much the same in every town. Why was that true?

The planners who built towns had many reasons for coming to Nebraska. They led the way for changes to happen. Towns attracted people of all nationalities and races. Towns attracted people with different skills. Blacksmiths, carpenters, printers, bakers, lawyers, doctors, teachers, and others came to the newly established towns of Nebraska to chase their dreams.

Cowtowns

Some planners were "steered" to Nebraska in pursuit of another kind of dream. Those dreams had their roots in the days of European colonies. In Chapter Four you read about the Europeans who came to the new world and established colonies. Do you remember the Spanish? They are the Europeans who founded the colonies in Mexico and Texas. The Spanish brought horses and cattle to their colonies. You already know how the horses brought by the Spanish changed the lives of the native people. The cattle brought by the Spanish also played a role in Nebraska's story.

The Spanish brought long-horned cattle to their colonies. These animals survived well in Texas and their numbers increased. Some dream chasers went to Texas to raise and sell cattle, but they needed to find markets for their cattle. The big cities in the United States were located east of the Mississippi River. Cattle raisers discovered that an animal sold in Texas might bring $6.00. The same animal sold in Chicago could bring $50.00.

There was money to be made in the cattle business. The problem was how to get the animals from Texas to Chicago.

The building of the transcontinental railroads across Kansas and Nebraska offered a possible solution to the Texas cattle raisers. If a herd of cattle could be driven from Texas to a transcontinental railroad, the cattle could be loaded on railroad cars and shipped to Chicago. The Kansas Pacific Railroad had been built across Kansas. Texas cattle raisers began driving longhorns north along trails into Kansas. Soon Abilene, Kansas, became an important cowtown (see map). The Union Pacific Railroad was interested in the business of hauling Texas cattle. The Union Pacific offered to haul cattle to Chicago at a cheaper rate than the Kansas Pacific, and beginning in 1870 thousands of cattle were driven into Nebraska.

The first important cowtown along the Union Pacific line was Schuyler. Nearly 50,000 cattle were sold at Schuyler in the summer of 1870, but the farmers who had settled around Schuyler did not want the cattle crossing their fields and destroying their crops. So, in 1871, the cattle trail led to Kearney, but here again there was trouble. Fighting broke out between the cowhands who herded the cattle on the trail and the local people. By 1873, Ogallala became Nebraska's most important cowtown. Within a short time more than 100,000 head of cattle were being shipped out of Ogallala each year.

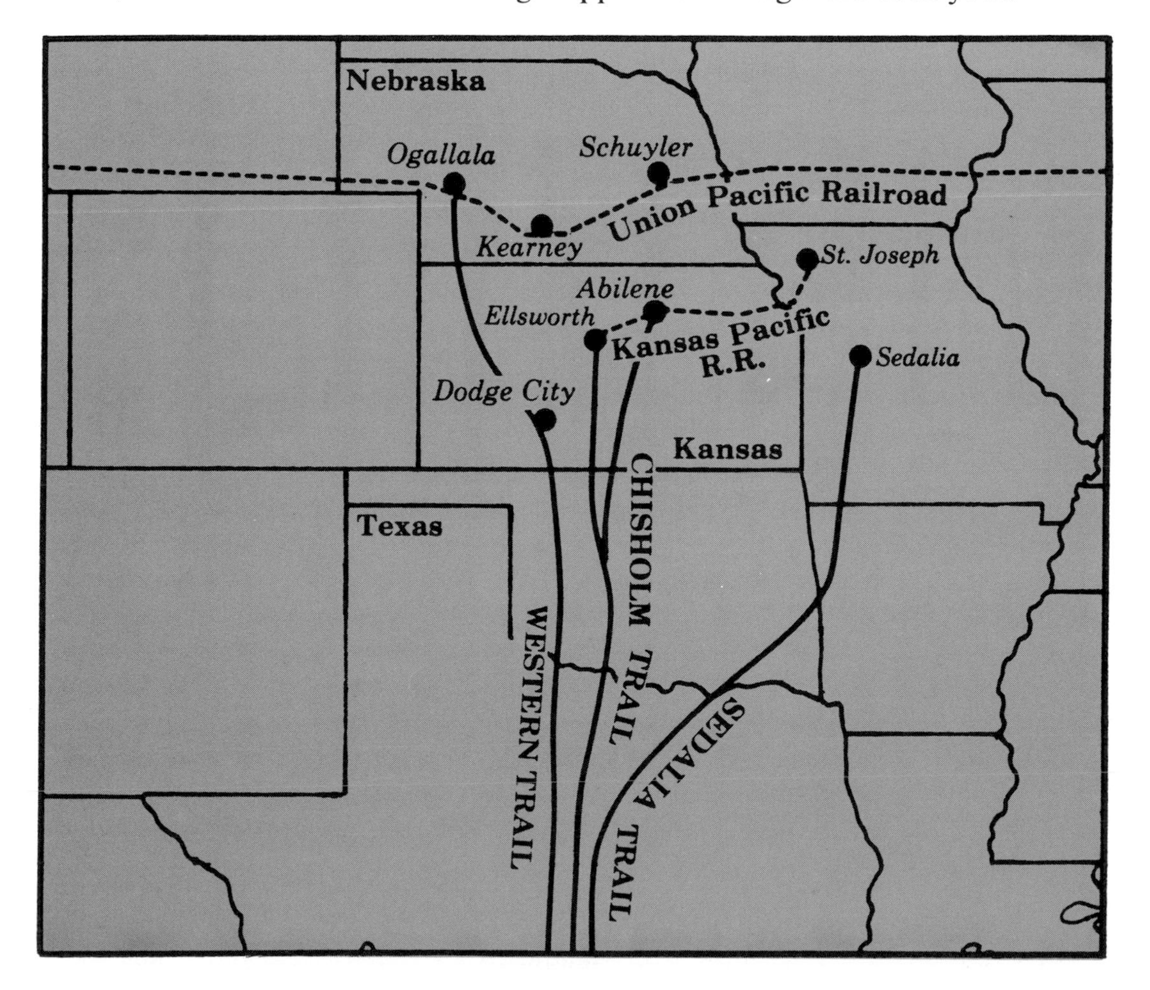

The cowhands who brought cattle to Ogallala were a tough lot. The cattle drives started in the spring. A small group of cowhands, maybe 12 to 15 in number, would round up a herd of 2,000 to 3,000 cattle. The trip from Texas to Nebraska took several months. The cowhands faced many dangers on the trail. Sometimes they met up with thieves who tried to steal cattle. There was always the danger of a stampede (STAM-PEDE) where the cattle would become frightened and run in all directions. Heavy spring thunderstorms could lead to swollen rivers and streams. The cattle had to be driven across the rivers and streams, and many a cowhand drowned while riding a horse across a dangerous stream.

When a cattle herd reached Ogallala, the cattle were sold to a buyer and the cowhands were paid in cash for their work. Having been on the trail for months, some cowhands celebrated too much. Gambling halls and saloons were common attractions to cowhands looking for a good time. There are stories told about cowhands who lost three months wages in a single night in the saloons of Ogallala.

Cattle Country

The cattle drives from Texas ended as quickly as they had begun. Settlers in western Kansas and Nebraska complained about the cattle destroying crops. By the mid-1880's, railroads were built across Texas and there was no longer a need to drive cattle north to Nebraska.

Photograph courtesy of Union Pacific Railroad Museum Collection

Photograph courtesy of Union Pacific Railroad Museum Collection

There were some dream chasers who recognized that western Nebraska was rich in grass. Much of the land belonged to the United States Government. If longhorns could thrive in Texas, would they not do well in Nebraska? Stories began to spread. A smart person, it was said, could turn cattle loose on the open range in western Nebraska. The cattle would feed on the grass until they were fat and then they could be sold for a large profit. Many dream chasers invested large sums of money in cattle hoping to get rich fast. Unfortunately, Nebraska's changeable weather brought a swift end to those dreams for some. Severe winter weather destroyed thousands of cattle in western Nebraska during the late 1880's.

Like the farmers, there were cattle raising dream chasers who would not give up. Many had obtained rich grasslands in the Sandhills. They put up fences on their land and began raising the finest cattle. The cattle business grew to become one of the most important businesses in Nebraska. In 1884, the Union Stock Yards Company was established in Omaha. Cattle from throughout Nebraska and neighboring states were shipped to Omaha. Big meat packing plants were established in Omaha. Here cattle were slaughtered and meat was shipped across the United States.

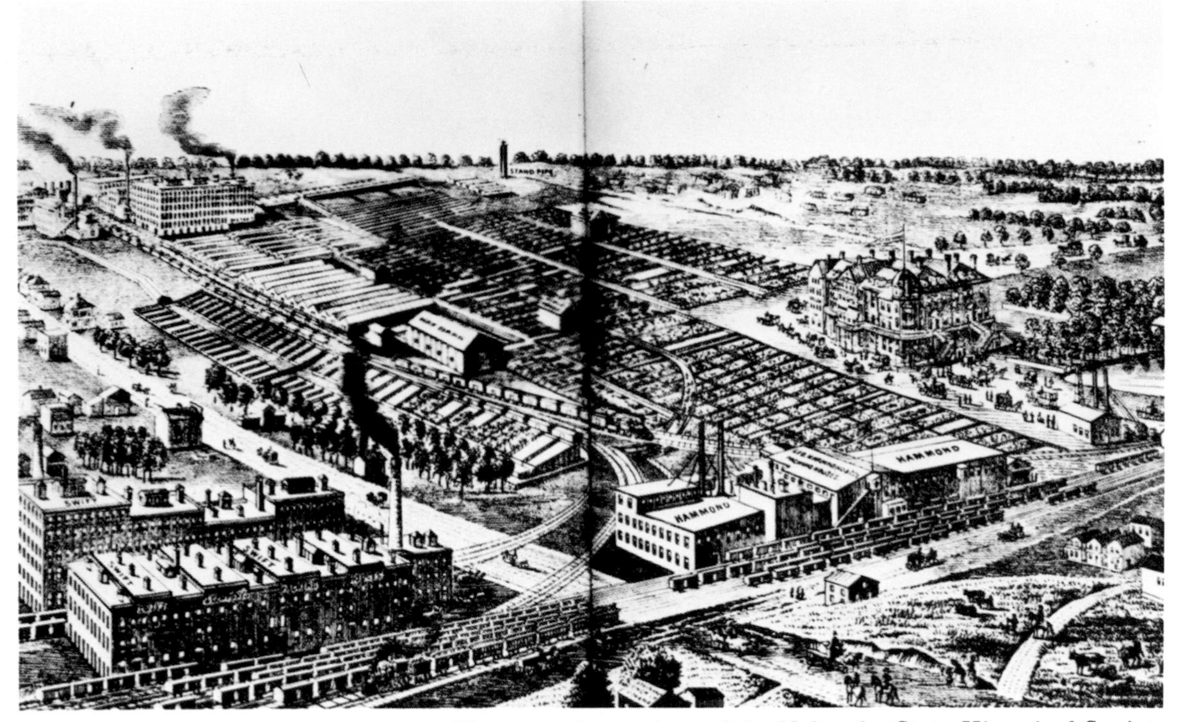

Photograph courtesy of the Nebraska State Historical Society

The Union Stock Yards Company of Omaha helped Omaha grow to become the world's largest cattle market and meat packer.

The meat packing and railroad businesses in Omaha attracted dream chasers from across the United States and the world. Thousands of black people moved from the south to find jobs in the meat and cattle business in Omaha. People migrated to Nebraska from Europe, Mexico, and Japan looking for work. The multiplying effect of change, where one change leads to many changes, began on the cattle trails leading to Nebraska in the 1870's. The cattle drives began a business that meant great change for Nebraska.

The Dream Chasers Transform Nebraska

Transform (TRANS-FORM) is a word that means to change. Thousands of dream chasers came to Nebraska following the Civil War and continued to come to Nebraska during the early 1900's. They came from every part of the world, but each individual came with a dream that was special to that person. With the dream chasers came different languages, customs, and beliefs. Their differences made them special, but their common efforts changed Nebraska. By the early 1900's, Nebraska was becoming a place where people farmed, ranched, and manufactured goods. It took hard work for the dream chasers to transform (TRANS-FORM) Nebraska, but they left a heritage for all Nebraskans. The heritage that courage and hard work can make dreams come true is something that belongs to you.

Important Ideas to Remember from the Dream Chasers—Part II

People of all races, creeds, and colors are dreamers.

Dream chasers by the thousands came to Nebraska following the Civil War.

One group of dream chasers, called planners, came to Nebraska to build towns and communities.

Some planners wanted to make money by building towns and communities. Other planners wanted to build towns and communities for people who shared a common set of beliefs or a common heritage.

Early towns in Nebraska looked much the same in appearance.

As the early towns grew, they attracted other dream chasers with many different skills and talents.

Another group of dream chasers brought cattle from Texas to Nebraska in the 1870's. They had dreams of getting rich by using the transcontinental railroads to ship Texas cattle to markets east of the Mississippi River.

Important cowtowns grew up along the Union Pacific Railroad in Nebraska.

Ogallala became the most important cowtown in Nebraska during the 1870's and 1880's.

Many dream chasers invested in cattle raising during the 1880's by buying cattle and allowing them to graze on the open range in western Nebraska.

The severe winter weather in Nebraska, and a new law dealing with enclosing public land, brought an end to open range cattle raising in the late 1880's.

Other dream chasers purchased Sandhills grassland, fenced it, and began raising high quality cattle.

The cattle business grew to become one of the most important businesses in Nebraska.

By the early 1900's, dream chasers from all around the world had come to Nebraska.

The dream chasers had transformed Nebraska into a place where farming, ranching, and manufacturing were important.

The dream chasers have left all Nebraskans with the heritage that courage and hard work can help make dreams come true.

Things to Do

1. Follow the trail of the dream chasers by using these guide words:
   YOUR TOWN (Look up anything you can find about the history and development of your town)
   LONG-HORNED CATTLE
   CHISHOLM TRAIL
   WESTERN TRAIL

CATTLE DRIVES
ABILENE
OGALLALA
UNION STOCK YARDS COMPANY
ETHNIC HERITAGE

2. Fun with numbers. You have been reading about the great changes made by the dream chasers as they came to Nebraska in the late 1800's and early 1900's. On the next page you will find some population information about Nebraska during this period. The information is shown in two forms. You will find a table which gives specific population figures by decade over a fifty-year period. The other form is a line graph which shows the same population information. Graphs and tables are useful tools. You can use the information they offer for a variety of purposes. Answer the following questions and then make up more questions to try out on your classmates.

Working With the Graph

a. In which decade did Nebraska's population change the most?
b. In which decade did Nebraska's population change the least?
c. A difficult question (think hard and list all the reasons that come to your mind): Why do you think Nebraska's population grew faster between the twenty-year period 1870 to 1890 than it did between the twenty-year period 1890 to 1910?
d. Project the graph out to the present time. How has Nebraska's population changed since 1910? Has Nebraska's population continued to grow? Plot on the graph what you think Nebraska's population was for each decade after 1910 up to the present.
e. After you have made your projections (guesses) and plotted them on the graph, you need to use your library skills and locate population figures for Nebraska. Record your population figures on the table. Now go back and plot the actual population figures on the graph. How accurate was your guess?

Working With the Table

a. What was the total change in Nebraska's population between 1860 and 1910?
b. If you have already done your library search and found population figures for each decade since 1910, answer this question. What is the total change in Nebraska's population since 1910?
c. Take a guess. Put a figure down for Nebraska's population fifty years from now. Why did you select that figure?

3. You know that many dream chasers came to Nebraska in the late 1800's and early 1900's. Are dream chasers still coming to Nebraska? If so, what kinds of dreams are the dream chasers pursuing? How will the new dream chasers change Nebraska?

Year	Population of Nebraska
1860	28,841
1870	122,993
1880	452,402
1890	1,058,910
1900	1,066,910
1910	1,192,214

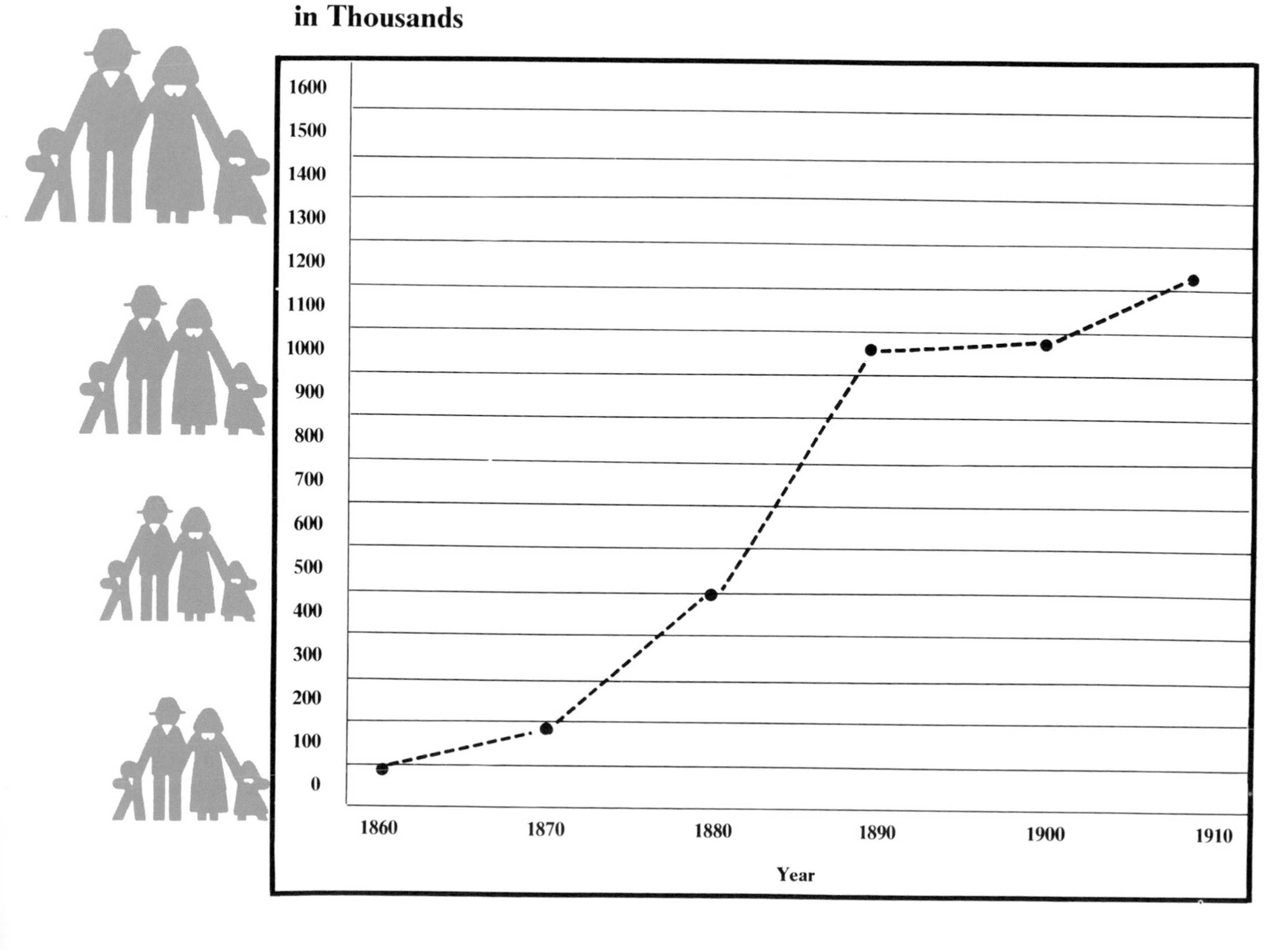

CHAPTER FIFTEEN

THE GREAT TRANSITION

Getting the Idea

Have you ever observed a caterpillar make a cocoon and eventually leave the cocoon as a butterfly? If you have made such an observation, you have seen a transition (TRAN-SI-TION). A worm turning into a butterfly is called a transition (TRAN-SI-TION). Transition is another name for change. It means that over time something has changed from one form to another form. The same pond that you fish in during the summer, you may skate on during the winter. Again, a transition has taken place. The water near the surface has changed over time from a liquid state to a solid state. The colder temperatures of winter helped to bring about the transition. Just for fun, make a list of the transitions you have observed or know about. Remember, for a transition to happen, something must change from one form to another form over time.

A great transition started in Nebraska during the late 1800's and the early 1900's. It took a period of time for this transition to happen. During this transition period, Nebraska changed from a frontier state into a modern state.

The dream chasers had come to Nebraska, and through hard work they established towns, farms, ranches, businesses, railroads, and roads. As you already know, the efforts of the dream chasers created great change. The railroads brought many people to Nebraska. Farms and ranches were started. Open prairies which once supported great buffalo herds and the Horse and Buffalo Culture of the native people were fenced. Farming and ranching became important businesses in Nebraska. The village people had raised a few crops for food. The newcomers raised crops and animals to sell. The native people had lived in scattered camps and villages. They came together in larger numbers to hunt the buffalo. Many newcomers lived in cities and towns. They lived and worked together in larger numbers the year round.

The new way people lived and worked in Nebraska meant that transportation and communication were more important than ever. Railroads were an excellent means of transportation. Railroads could be used to transport people to Nebraska and within Nebraska. Railroads could also be used to transport crops and animals in and out of Nebraska. It was also necessary to develop a system of roads. Farmers and ranchers had to be able to travel to nearby towns to sell their goods and to buy supplies and needed services. People in towns and cities depended upon roads to link their communities with other communities.

A new age was beginning in Nebraska, and that new age brought change at a faster rate. Keep in mind the "multiplier effect" for change. One important change usually leads to many changes. As changes happen over time, they happen at a faster rate.

The Modern Force for Change

Think back over Nebraska's story. Over a period of millions of years Nebraska was shaped by the forces of nature. Water, wind, ice, great up-liftings from the earth, and climate were some of the tools used by nature to create the place we know as Nebraska. The great hunters came to Nebraska, but they made few significant changes. The native people occupied Nebraska for many years. They established a way of life in which they lived through the gifts of nature by hunting, gathering, and farming. The horse gave great mobility to the native people and became a most important means of change for the native culture.

Think-Tank Time

When the dream chasers entered Nebraska they brought a new force for change. Look at the following list of inventions. What made these inventions possible? What was the great force for change that was at work at this time? How do you think that force for change made life different for the people in Nebraska?

Invention	Year
Telegraph	1837
Barbed Wire	1874
Telephone	1876
Disc Cultivator	1878
Electric Trolley	1884
Phonograph	1887
American Steam Automobile	1889
American Gasoline Automobile	1892
Airplane	1903

Did you guess the great force for change to be science? Maybe you think of science as a subject to learn. Science is really a way of learning! When people employ science to learn they ask questions, they observe, they accurately collect information, they make guesses, they conduct experiments to test their ideas, and they try to keep an open mind. Through science, this way of learning, people gain knowledge. The knowledge gained through science is used to make new discoveries and to invent new machines. The more people learn through science, the more change that happens. The more change that happens, the faster the rate of change. The use of science as a way of learning became the most important force for change in Nebraska after the arrival of the dream chasers.

The Big Change

Science was not invented in Nebraska. This important way of learning was brought to Nebraska by the dream chasers. When you compare life in Nebraska before and after the arrival of the dream chasers, you get some idea of how science became the great force for change. The native people had a rich and beautiful culture, but it was not a scientific culture. The native people had no written language. They were an oral people. Stories and information were passed on from older people to younger people. Elders were given special respect in tribal groups because of the wisdom they had gained through life. It was believed that some tribal members had special powers. Within many tribes, clans or groups of individuals had certain duties which only they could perform. For the native people, it was most important to look to the past and to the customs that had been established over time. These were the things that gave direction and made life predictable.

After the arrival of the dream chasers, a scientific culture was set in place. The newcomers immediately set up schools. Information and ideas were passed on between old and young through a written language. The newcomers also established colleges and universities. Located in Lincoln, the University of Nebraska, in particular, became a place where science was used to gain much knowledge. Although the past was important to the newcomers, there were always people willing to accept the new ideas, the new discoveries, and the new inventions of science. It was the knowledge gained from science that gave direction to life. Science also made life much less predictable. For better or for worse, by the early 1900's the people of Nebraska came to accept the idea that change through science was going to be an important and constant part of their lives.

Important Ideas to Remember from the Great Transition

Transition is a word that means change. Over time, some things can change from one form to another form.

During the late 1800's and early 1900's a great transition took place in Nebraska. Nebraska was changed from a frontier state to a modern state.

Science was and continues to be the great force for change in modern Nebraska.

Science is a way of learning.

In learning through science people ask questions, make observations, collect information, make guesses, conduct experiments, and keep open minds.

Through science much knowledge is discovered and used.

The use of science as a way of learning brings about more changes at a faster rate.

Things to Do

1. Instead of a list of guide words, follow these topics to your nearest library for some interesting reading.
   A. Agriculture. You should be able to find lots of information about how science has changed agriculture since the late 1800's. In particular look for information on machines and new sources of power in agriculture. You might also look for information on how science has been used to improve the raising of plants and animals. You might also find some differing points of view about the use of science in agriculture. Does everyone agree that the use of chemicals in modern agriculture is a good thing?
   B. Transportation. How has science changed transportation? How have the changes in transportation made Nebraska a different place from what it was when it became a state in 1867? How might future changes in transportation affect Nebraska?
   C. Communication. What are the most common forms of communication in the world today? When did these forms of communication come into existence? How does modern communication affect life in Nebraska today? Are there new forms of communication that might make life different in the future?

2. People have beliefs that usually come to them from the past. Sometimes science brings new knowledge or discoveries that challenge people's beliefs. For example, at one time many people believed the earth to be the center of the universe. Science challenged that belief by offering new knowledge that the earth was part of the solar system and orbited the sun. When this happened there was conflict between science and personal beliefs. Here are some hard questions to think about. Do science and beliefs still conflict today? Can you find some examples in the news to show that science and beliefs can be in conflict at times? In your opinion, is it good or bad that science and beliefs can conflict at times?

CHAPTER SIXTEEN
HAPPY DAYS

Prosperity

Prosperity (PROS-PER-I-TY) is a word that means successful or well-off. A prosperous (PROS-PER-OUS) person is one who has been successful and is able to enjoy some wealth. Do you know any prosperous people?

One way to measure prosperity (PROS-PER-I-TY) is by income, that is how much money a person earns. Another way to measure prosperity is by the value of property or goods owned. Prosperous people often own property like houses, land, machines, businesses, and other things that may be worth much money. Scientists called economists (ECON-O-MISTS) often study how prosperous a state or a country is at a point in time. For example, here is some information economists (ECON-O-MISTS) have collected about Nebraska in the early 1900's. Compare the information from the year 1900 with that of 1910.

What can you see by comparing the figures from 1900 with those of 1910? There were more farms in Nebraska in 1910 than in 1900. The machinery, buildings, land, and animals on the farms were worth more money. There were also more manufacturing businesses in Nebraska. Those businesses employed more workers who made more products that were worth more money.

On the Farm

Measure of Prosperity	1900	1910
	(Rounded Figures)	
Number of Farms	122,000	130,000
Value of Farm Land & Buildings	$578,000,000	$1,800,000,000
Value of Farm Machinery	$25,000,000	$44,000,000
Value of Livestock	$145,000,000	$222,000,000

Manufacturing

Measure of Prosperity	1900	1910
	(Rounded Figures)	
Number of Businesses	1,700	2,500
Number of Workers	19,000	25,000
Value of Goods Produced	$93,000,000	$199,000,000

Challenge

Life in Nebraska was changing. In general, during the early 1900's people in Nebraska were becoming more prosperous than they had been in earlier years. Before reading further, take a piece of paper and list some reasons you think people were becoming more prosperous during this time in Nebraska's history. Be ready to discuss your ideas with your classmates.

Listing and Discussing

Your teacher can serve as the recorder for this exercise, writing your ideas on the chalkboard. Every person in the class gets to offer one reason why he/she thinks Nebraskans were becoming more properous in the early 1900's than they had been in earlier years. When you have finished talking about your ideas and have recorded them on the chalkboard, finish reading the chapter. Continue to compare your ideas with those found in the remaining part of the chapter.

Science

Did your class identify science as one reason for the growth in Nebraska's prosperity during this period? Science, the important way of discovering new knowledge, had much to do with Nebraska's growing prosperity in the early 1900's. Science made possible new labor-saving machines that were used in farming. Steam machines and gasoline-fueled tractors began to replace horses and mules on the farm. The new machines of the 1900's saved time and labor. Farmers could farm more land and earn more money.

Photograph courtesy of the Nebraska State Historical Society

STEAM THRESHER

After wheat had been cut and dried, farmers used threshing machines to separate the wheat from the straw. Threshing was hard work, but easier than separating wheat from straw by hand.

Photograph courtesy of the Nebraska State Historical Society

GANG PLOW

The huge steam tractor pulled the gang plow which was used to turn large amounts of sod. Think how much easier this was than breaking sod with oxen as was done in the pioneer days.

Science also made possible the development of an important new crop for Nebraska farmers. When the dream chasers first settled Nebraska, they grew wheat that was planted in the spring. Spring wheat never grew well in Nebraska. Scientists at the University of Nebraska experimented with growing a different kind of wheat that was planted in the winter. Winter wheat, developed through the efforts of university scientists, became an important crop. Nebraska became a leading wheat growing state and Nebraska farmers prospered.

Other scientific work done at the University of Nebraska meant greater prosperity for Nebraska farmers. A special drug was developed to prevent a disease known as hog cholera (CHOL-ER-A). This terrible disease killed many hogs. After the hog cholera drug was developed, farmers raised and sold many more hogs.

University of Nebraska scientists worked with farmers to improve cattle raising. Dairy farming became big business. University of Nebraska scientists and state veterinarians traveled across the state teaching farmers to use new knowledge gained from science to become more prosperous.

Science also changed the way people lived and worked in towns and cities. Steam and electricity were used to drive new machines. Like on the farm, new machines meant one person could do more work in less time.

Photograph courtesy of the Nebraska State Historical Society

OMAHA CUDAHY PLANT AT TURN OF THE CENTURY
Omaha continued to grow as Nebraska's largest city. The meat packing industry employed many workers and used new machines and modern transportation.

The automobile was another important invention that helped change life in Nebraska. Reportedly, the first automobile in Nebraska appeared on the streets of Nebraska City in 1895. By 1902, the streets of Lincoln were visited by these noisy inventions. Prosperous Nebraskans continued to buy automobiles, and in 1905 the Legislature passed a law to control their use. Most people used horses for local transportation. Automobiles were noisy and frightened horses. The 1905 law required automobile operators to stop their machine and allow frightened horses to pass.

Photograph courtesy Solomon D. Butcher Collection, Nebraska State Historical Society

MAIN STREET MERNA IN 1910
The automobile was changing Nebraska by the early 1900's. Notice the sign over the livery garage offers "automobile and machine work."

Some Things to Think About

When the automobile was first invented, many people regarded it as a toy. Some people said the automobile would never replace the horse. A few people bought automobiles in the early 1900's, but they often used them for pleasure driving on weekends. Modern change happens quickly! Look at the figures below. They show the growing number of automobiles owned in Nebraska over a twenty-five year period.

Year	Automobiles in Nebraska
1905	571
1920	205,000
1930	367,410

The line graph on the next page shows the same figures used in the table above.

1. In your opinion, why did the automobile become so popular so quickly in Nebraska?
2. In what ways do you think the automobile changed the way people lived in Nebraska?
3. Do you think the line on the line graph continued to climb sharply? Would there be a time when the line would level off? Why or why not? What can you do to find out?
4. Is the use of the automobile like other changes brought about by science? Can you think of other inventions or discoveries which have quickly changed the way people lived? Remember, in 1852 people were traveling across Nebraska in wagons pulled by oxen and horses. In 1902, fifty years later, a few people were driving cars in the capital city!
5. The automobile was regarded as useless by many people when it first became available. Soon people changed their minds. Today the automobile is regarded by most Americans as essential, something people cannot get along without. In your opinion, why do people often find it hard to accept something that is new or different?

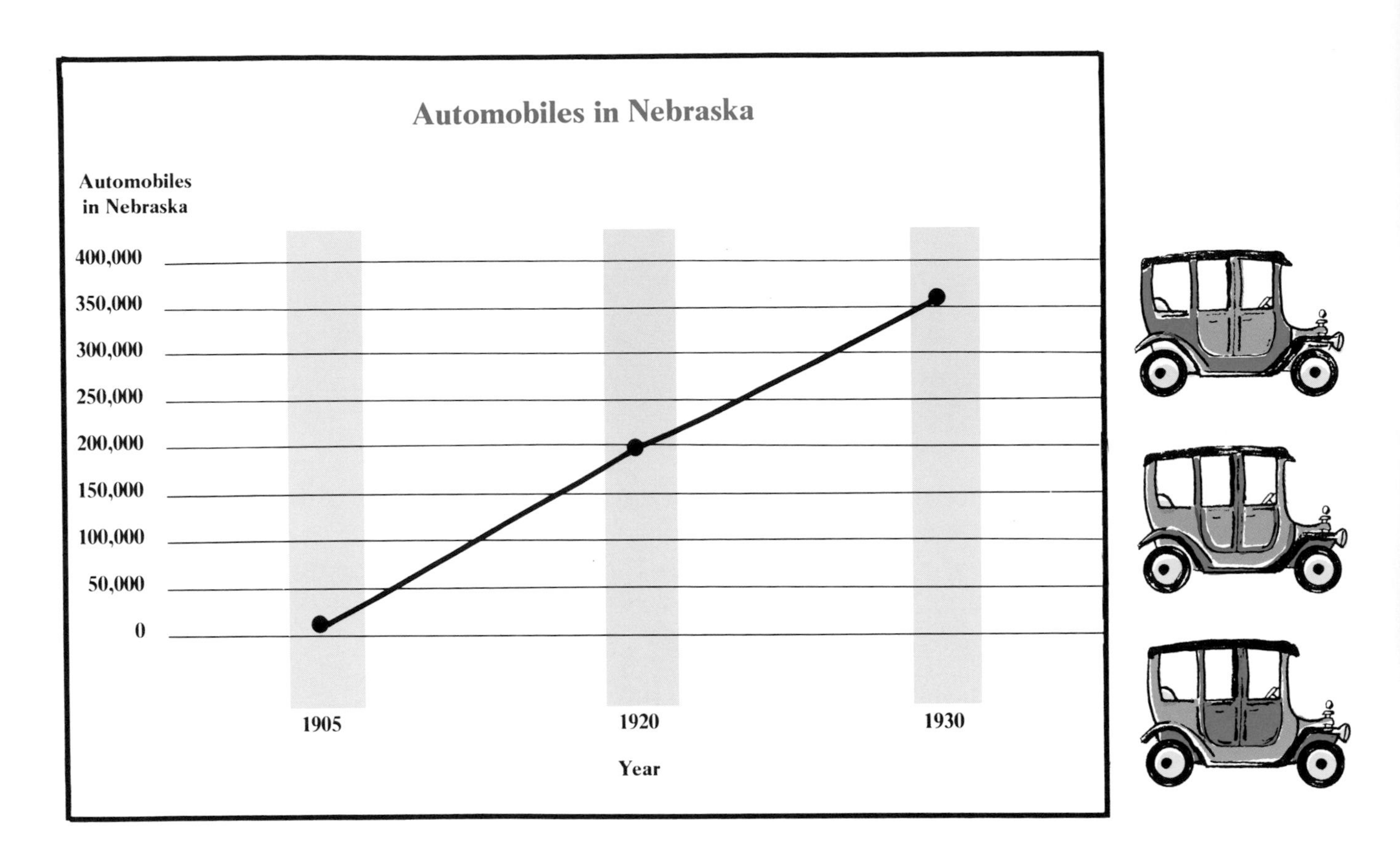

Prosperity Grows

Science helped to make Nebraskans prosperous in the early 1900's, and nature added its touch. There were no more grasshopper invasions like those of earlier years. More important, there was plenty of rain across the state. Good rain years meant good crop years. If crops were good, farmers and others were prosperous.

It seemed as if science and nature were working together to make Nebraska that rich and beautiful place the railroads had promised when they encouraged immigrants to move to Nebraska after the Civil War. These were good times. The dream chasers seemed to be right. A person could make dreams come true in Nebraska.

Important Ideas to Remember from Happy Days

Prosperity is a word that means successful or well-off.

In the early 1900's, Nebraskans were more prosperous than they had been in the past.

- The inventions and discoveries made through science were changing the way people lived in Nebraska by the early 1900's. People were using the knowledge gained from science to live more properous lives.
- The automobile was one of the most important inventions brought to Nebraska during the early 1900's. The automobile became the most common form of transportation used in Nebraska. The automobile greatly changed how people lived in Nebraska.
- In the early 1900's, nature cooperated with science in making Nebraska a more prosperous place to live.

Things to Do

1. Why not prosper by following these guide words to your nearest library? There is a wealth of information to be found. It will make your life richer.

   AGRICULTURE
   WINTER WHEAT
   SPRING WHEAT
   THRESHERS
   PLOWS
   TRACTORS
   IRRIGATION
   DRY LAND FARMING
   INDUSTRIAL REVOLUTION
   AUTOMOBILE
   HENRY FORD

2. ASSIGNMENT PROBE. Probe means to examine. Have your ever been to a dentist? If so, you know the dentist will put instruments in your mouth as he/she examines your teeth. These instruments are called probes. Probes allow the dentist to get into hard to see places to make certain that you have no decay or cavities in those places.

   Your assignment is to probe your community. Find evidence of how the automobile changed your community. You can interview people. You can locate old photographs and maps. You can examine buildings (if allowed). You can scour old newspapers. (The local library may be a good place for finding old newspapers.) You can even check when the nearest drive-in theater or drive-in restaurant was built. When you have finished your probe, you will have first-hand evidence of change brought through science. That same power for change continues in your life today!

CHAPTER SEVENTEEN
WORLD WAR

War Breaks Out

Science, nature, and hard work continued to bring prosperity to Nebraska in the early years of the twentieth century. (Century means 100-year periods of time. The twentieth century means the twentieth 100-year period since the birth of Christ.) New inventions and discoveries changed life in Nebraska while nature offered healthy amounts of sunshine and rain.

Some ugly clouds did gather on the horizon by 1914, but these were clouds of war and not a threat from nature. The nations of Europe, just as they had done in earlier history, entered into a great rivalry. The nations of Europe had established colonies all over the world. Each nation wanted to become rich and powerful. This time the nations of Great Britain, France, and Russia (the Allies) found themselves opposing the nations of Germany, Austria-Hungary, Bulgaria, and Turkey (the Central Powers) (see map).

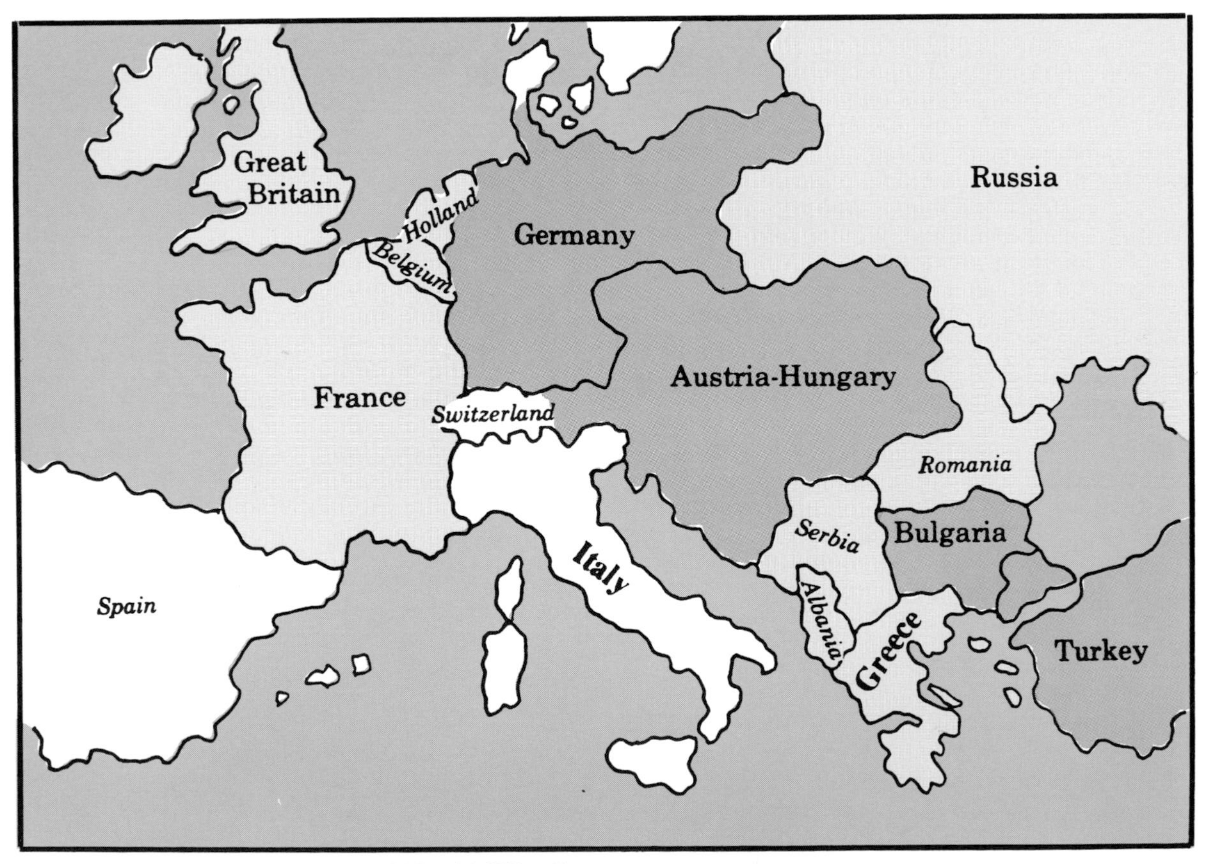

Europe at the outbreak of World War I.

The Allies had made secret agreements to help each other in case of conflict with the Central Powers. The Central Powers had made similar agreements to stand together against the Allies. A great war broke out between the Allies and the Central Powers in July, 1914. Eventually, nations from all over the world entered into what became known as World War I. The United States entered World War I in April, 1917. The war ended in November, 1918, after great loss of life and property.

From Neutrality to War

When World War I broke out, Woodrow Wilson was President of the United States. President Wilson promised that the United States would remain neutral (not take sides) in the war. Although some people had great feelings about the war, most Nebraskans thought the United States should not take sides and should stay out of the war.

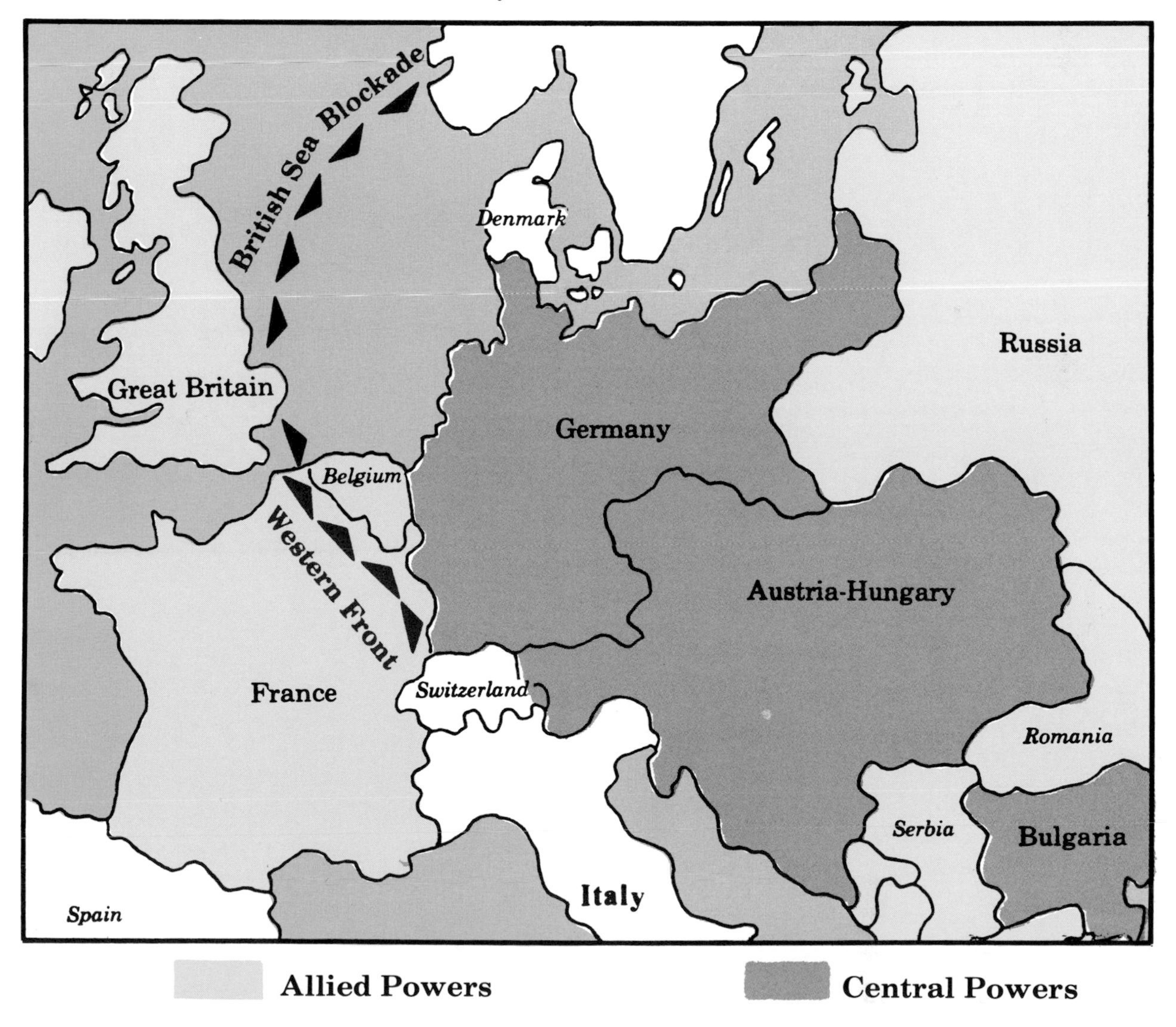

As the war continued, it became clear that neither the Allies nor the Central Powers could win the war easily. Soldiers on the western front dug a network of trenches over 600 miles in length that stretched across France and Belgium (see map). Thousands of soldiers lived in these trenches. Sometimes the trenches of the Allies and the Central Powers were only a few yards apart. The trenches protected the soldiers from enemy bullets. Between the trenches was an area called "no man's land." Conditions on the western front were terrible. When it rained, water filled the trenches. Rats infested the trenches and life on the western front was miserable.

New knowledge discovered through science can be used for good and/or evil. In World War I, the leaders of nations used science to invent weapons for killing and destruction. The airplane, an invention of the twentieth century, was used for bombing and strafing. In strafing, machine guns were placed in airplanes. The airplanes flew low over enemy troops and machine gun bullets were sprayed over the area. Other terrible weapons were developed. Huge cannons were invented. These big guns could hurl deadly shells over 75 miles. The tank, a heavy motorized weapon, was invented and used during World War I. One of the most deadly weapons of World War I was used on the oceans.

Great Britain had a large navy and used its ships to blockade important German seaports (see map). The Germans used submarines to sink the ships of the Allies. The Germans also sank the ships of other nations in order to prevent the Allies from receiving needed war supplies. During World War I, passenger ships sailed between the United States and Europe. Sometimes war supplies were loaded on to these ships. The Germans warned Americans not to travel on passenger ships that sailed into war zones. In 1915, a German submarine sank a ship named the Lusitania, killing 128 Americans. Many Americans were angry over German submarine attacks.

By 1917, Americans had become more willing to support the Allies. Finally, on April 6, 1917, the United States declared war on Germany and entered the war on the side of the Allies.

Nebraskans at War

Once the United States entered World War I, Nebraskans helped in important ways to bring about victory for the Allies. It took large amounts of money for the United States Government to create a fighting force. Soldiers, sailors, and pilots had to be trained. Weapons, ships, airplanes, and uniforms had to be made. The government asked people to buy liberty bonds. In buying a bond, a person loaned money to the government. The government promised to pay the money back at a later time. Nebraskans bought thousands of liberty bonds to help the government obtain money to fight the war.

One of the most important contributions Nebraskans made was in providing food for the Allies. Nebraska farmers planted more crops and produced more food than ever before. A large amount of grassland in western Nebraska was plowed and planted to wheat. The war brought greater prosperity to Nebraska. The more farmers produced, the greater their prosperity. Look at the tables below. What do they tell you about prosperity in Nebraska during World War I?

Three Important Crops in Nebraska

Corn

Year	Price per Bushel	Bushels Produced
1917	$1.20	223,500,000
1918	$1.28	123,300,000
1919	$1.22	182,251,000

Oats

Year	Price per Bushel	Bushels Produced
1917	.61	117,000,000
1918	.65	56,215,000
1919	.65	70,134,000

Wheat

Year	Price per Bushel	Bushels Produced
1917	$1.95	12,603,000
1918	$1.97	43,242,000
1919	$2.02	61,235,000

You can see from the tables that the prices paid for all three crops improved between 1917 and 1919, although the price of corn did fall between 1918 and 1919. You can see from the tables that Nebraska farmers grew more wheat and that the price of wheat continued to go up during the war. The Allies needed wheat to make bread, a basic food for soldiers and the hungry people in Europe.

The Great Sacrifice

The price of war is always great. What value can be placed on a human life? Nebraskans were called upon in World War I to join the fighting forces of the Allies. Of the 57,526 Nebraska men and women who served in the American armed forces during World War I, 1,655 were killed or wounded.

When the war ended in November, 1918, there were great celebrations. However, millions of people had died. Millions of people had been crippled or injured in the war. The war had cost large amounts of money to fight. Between 1914 and 1917, World War I cost about $85,000 per minute to fight. In 1918, the cost of the war rose to about $170,000 per minute. (Use a calculator. Figure how much money it cost to fight World War I. How do you figure the cost?) Was the war worth the cost of lives, property, and money? Is war ever worth the price people must pay?

The Price

I am ready to fight.
My country is right.
Destroy the enemy.
Pay no heed to the cries for mercy.

The days are long.
Could I be wrong?
Both sides bleed.
Pity those who have lost their loved ones.

What have we done?
Curse those with guns.
Time has come.
Let there be peace on earth forever more.

War is like a disease without a cure. It is a terrible thing when people set out with weapons to injure or kill other people. Why does this happen? You already know that the Europeans fought wars during the colonial days. Each European country wanted to become rich and powerful. The native people in Nebraska fought wars. During the Horse and Buffalo Culture, a man proved his bravery through acts of war. Soldiers of the United States Army fought the native people in Nebraska and in the surrounding area. The Government of the United States wanted to take the land promised to the native people as well as to destroy the Horse and Buffalo Culture. Why do wars happen? Can wars be prevented?

Eliminating War

Eliminate means to get rid of something. How can people eliminate war? If you think about disease, you know that scientists cannot find ways to eliminate a disease until the cause of the disease is known. Once the cause is understood, science can be used to help find a cure for the disease. The same is true for war. If war is to be eliminated, people must understand the causes of war and then be willing to treat those causes.

Plan for Action

There is nothing more important than the elimination of war. Killing and destruction are the goals of war.

1. Think about what you have read in *Changing Nebraska*. Take a piece of paper and write down your ideas. What do you think are some causes of war?
2. Hold a class discussion. Every person needs to speak. From this discussion, get a list of ideas about the causes of war.
3. Examine the list of causes your class has put together. For each cause, determine what you can do as a person to eliminate war. State what you think your class can do as a group to eliminate war.

The following example may help you in your planning.

Cause

A cause of war is ignorance.

Individual Action

I will learn as much as I can about the world and other people.
I will keep an open mind. I will always seek information to help me better understand issues and problems.

Group Action

We can write letters to our principal, superintendent of schools, and to our school board. In our letters, we can ask those who make decisions about our school to do more in teaching students how to solve conflicts. (The elimination of war begins with knowing how to live together with your neighbors and friends.)

Our class can pledge that all members will make an effort to better understand and respect one another. Hint—You will have to come up with some ideas for your class to act upon in order to fulfill the pledge.

The Great Change Brought by World War

When World War I ended, the people of Nebraska were happy. There seemed to be general agreement that World War I was the war to end all wars. The feeling against war was strong. Nebraskans were ready to forget the war and to get back to a life of peaceful prosperity. A basic change had taken place, however, and life in Nebraska would never be the same.

Before World War I, Nebraskans had been caught up in the job of making dreams come true. The dream chasers had come to Nebraska to make a new life. People came to Nebraska from all over the world. They worked hard, and Nebraska had become a more prosperous place.

During World War I, Nebraskans had to turn their attention to the job of winning the war. They produced food for the Allies. They sent men and women to Europe to serve in the war. The people of Nebraska had become citizens of the world. The people of Nebraska found that what happened in faraway places did affect them. Through the inventions and discoveries of science, the people of the world were brought closer together. This important change means that all of the people in the world are your brothers and sisters. What happens to others, no matter where they might live, has importance for you.

Important Ideas to Remember from World War

The nations of Europe entered into a great war in July, 1914.

The nations of Great Britain, France, and Russia (the Allies) opposed the nations of Germany, Austria-Hungary, Bulgaria, and Turkey (the Central Powers).

The United States refused to take sides in the war. Most people in Nebraska thought that the United States should stay out of the war.

New knowledge gained from science made World War I a horrible war. New weapons were invented and millions of people were killed and injured.

In April, 1917, the United States entered World War I on the side of the Allies.

Nebraskans helped in the war effort by buying liberty bonds, by raising crops and animals to be used for food, and by sending over 50,000 men and women to serve in the armed forces.

World War I brought great change to Nebraska. The people of Nebraska were caught up in world affairs beyond the borders of Nebraska. After World War I, it was no longer possible for Nebraskans to ignore what was happening in other parts of the world.

The inventions and discoveries of science had made the people of the world more dependent on one another.

Things to Do

1. Your library is full of rich reading material dealing with this important time in Nebraska's history. A few guide words can lead you to many interesting discoveries.

   WORLD WAR I
   WOODROW WILSON
   ALLIES
   CENTRAL POWERS
   SUBMARINE WARFARE
   LUSITANIA
   TRENCH WARFARE

2. Your life is linked with the lives of people around the world. No matter where you live in Nebraska, you depend upon people from all over the globe. Project International will help you identify the ties that link your community to the world.

   Project International is a class search of your community by you and your classmates. You are to look for all the ways you can discover which show that the people in your community are citizens of the world. The first thing you need to do is to hold a class discussion. Your class can brainstorm a list of categories or areas that can be explored. Next, people need to be assigned to each area or category.

Following the class discussion and assignments, you can decide how you will collect your information. Any method of information collection is fair, just be sure that everyone brings back evidence. You may take notes, you may take photographs, you may make audio and/or visual tape recordings, or you may do any other kind of information collecting that can be used in your effort. Be sure to decide, as a group, how much time you will allow for the community information collection.

Once the information is collected, your class can draw and paint a large map of the world. Then using colored yarn, link your community to other places in the world. For example, if somebody found coffee in the grocery store that comes from Brazil, link your community to Brazil. If another person brought a photograph that shows an automobile that was made in Japan, link your community to Japan. You might also find evidence that things are shipped from your community or area to other places in the world. If you have evidence of such businesses, link your community to the places receiving local products. For example, you might find that your local mill operator sells grain that goes to Russia.

When you have finished linking your community with the world, invite your parents to your classroom to view your map. Your parents may be surprised to find how closely your community is tied to the rest of the world. We are family!

CHAPTER EIGHTEEN
ROAD TO HARDSHIP

The Good and the Bad

Have you been to a party or to a special event where there was a lot of food and drink? While at such an event, have you ever had too much to eat and drink?

Personal note from the author—When I was about eight years old a neighbor woman gave a party for her parents. Her parents celebrated their golden wedding anniversary (50 years of marriage). The entire neighborhood was invited to the party. I found that I could have all the soda pop and food I wanted. Within a short time, I had eaten cake, sandwiches, chips, cookies, nuts, and drank twelve bottles of soda pop. I had a great time, but needless to say, I got sick to my stomach that night. I learned a valuable lesson from that experience. I learned that good times can lead to bad consequences if you fail to use good judgment. Have you learned that lesson in your life? Think about it.

Good times, poor judgment, and bad consequences tell the story of changing Nebraska during the 1920's and 1930's. When World War I ended, Nebraskans like other Americans were ready to get back to normal. Remember, normal before and during World War I was a life of growing prosperity. The inventions and discoveries of science had made it possible for farmers and workers to produce more goods. The weather in Nebraska had been ideal for farmers. During the war, farmers enjoyed high prices for their goods. The more farmers produced, the more prosperity they enjoyed.

In some ways during the 1920's, there was every reason to believe prosperity would continue forever. Nebraskans bought more automobiles. Science had made it possible for people across the state to be connected by telephone networks. The people in towns and cities enjoyed electric lights and the use of modern electric appliances like washing machines and vacuum cleaners. Movie theaters had come into existence earlier, but in 1927 the first "talkies" were shown in Nebraska. Knowledge gained through science made it possible to have movies with sound! One of the most important inventions that gained widespread acceptance in Nebraska was radio. At first people made or bought crystal sets where they used earphones to hear radio broadcasts. Within a few years, receiving sets were developed and radio broadcasts were picked up without need of earphones. Radios became home entertainment centers. No matter where a person was located, news, music, and entertainment were available through radio. How would radio and telephones have made life different for the dream chasers who first settled Nebraska?

During the 1920's, radio began to bring news and entertainment into many Nebraska homes. Crystal sets, like the one in the picture, were used to receive radio signals. Home receivers (radios) became common within a few short years.

Photograph courtesy of the Nebraska State Historical Society

Movies were a popular form of entertainment in Nebraska towns during the 1920's. By 1927, movies with sound were available.

Photograph courtesy of the Nebraska State Historical Society

Tall buildings, automobiles, busy streets, and evidence of electricity and radio in this 1929 photograph of downtown Omaha reflect the prosperity of this time.

There were other signs of prosperity in Nebraska during the 1920's. More roads were constructed. The cities of Omaha and Lincoln grew, and tall buildings were erected in the downtown areas of those cities. One of the most important projects for all Nebraskans began in 1922. A decision had been made to build a new state capitol. After months of planning, ground was broken for the new capitol in November, 1922. It took ten years to complete construction. Nebraska's capitol is recognized as one of the most beautiful buildings in the world. The capitol stands as a tribute to the people of Nebraska.

Photograph courtesy of the Nebraska State Historical Society

Nebraska's new capitol as it appeared in 1928.

Despite all the signs of prosperity, the good times were based on poor judgment and bad consequences were assured. During the 1920's, Nebraskans depended upon agriculture for prosperity. (Agriculture has to do with all jobs related to the growing and selling of crops and livestock. Such jobs would include farming, ranching, seed supplying, meat packing, mill operating, etc.) The majority of Nebraskans lived on farms and ranches and in small towns. In the early 1900's, science, weather, and hard work had brought prosperity. During World War I, farmers were told to grow more crops. You already know that prices for crops were high during the war years. Farmers decided to borrow money from banks and buy more land. The more land a farmer owned, the more crops that could be produced. With modern machinery, it was possible for a single farmer to work more land. Farmers borrowed money to buy new farm machinery. The new machinery was expensive, but big crop production and high crop prices meant farmers could easily earn enough money to pay off loans.

Brain Teaser

Why do you think it may have been poor judgment for Nebraska's farmers to borrow large sums of money to buy land and machinery during the war years and the years immediately following World War I? Think hard about that question. The great change that came about as a result of World War I has caused serious problems for Nebraska's farmers and ranchers over the years. Understanding the great change helps to explain some of the difficulties faced by modern farmers and ranchers. Take plenty of time for class discussion.

Compounding Change

You remember the "multiplier effect" for change—important changes lead to other changes. You might also recall the idea about the speed of change. Change seems to happen faster as more changes occur. Another effect of change is the "compounding effect." That is, because important changes lead to other changes which happen faster, problems can sometimes become more difficult to solve. It becomes hard to sort through all the changes and their effects. Changes build upon one another in rapid fashion. This compounding is what has happened in agriculture.

When farmers used new knowledge from science, they found they could produce more crops. World War I came along and much farmland in Europe was taken out of production. European farmers could not grow crops on land located in war zones. Nebraska farmers could grow crops to send to Europe. The people in Europe needed food. When the war ended, European farmers went back to their fields and began farming again. By 1921, Europeans did not need wheat or corn from Nebraska because they grew their own. Unfortunately, farmers in Nebraska continued to raise large amounts of crops. They no longer had a place to sell all their crops. Since American farmers grew more than was needed, the prices for crops began to fall. Once prices fell, farmers earned less money. Since farmers earned less money, they found it difficult to pay back the money they had borrowed from banks. Banks that had loaned out money which could not be paid back went broke. The more banks that closed their doors, the more difficult it became for farmers to borrow money needed to plant crops. This "compounding effect" of change led to bad consequences.

Study the graphs on the next page. Think about what the graphs tell you. Now, consider this statement:

Poor Judgment

It was poor judgment by Nebraska farmers to produce more crops by borrowing money to buy land and machinery during and immediately after World War I.

Bad Consequences

Study the graphs and then on a piece of paper list three bad consequences that resulted from the poor judgment stated above. How do the consequences you list compare with the ideas your class discussed earlier in the Brain Teaser activity?

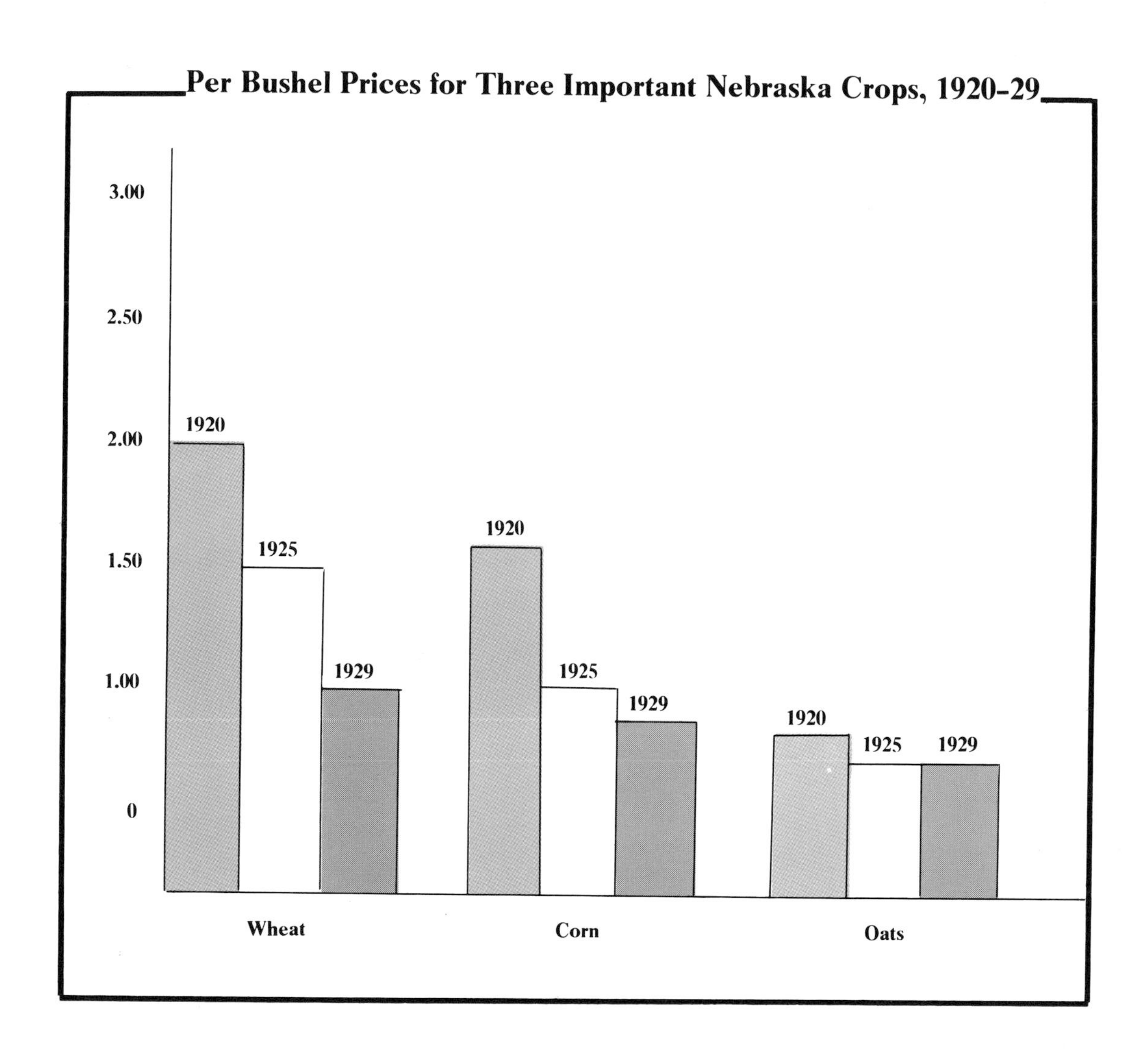
Per Bushel Prices for Three Important Nebraska Crops, 1920-29
3.00
2.50
2.00
1.50
1.00
0
1920
1925
1929
1920
1925
1929
1920
1925
1929
Wheat
Corn
Oats

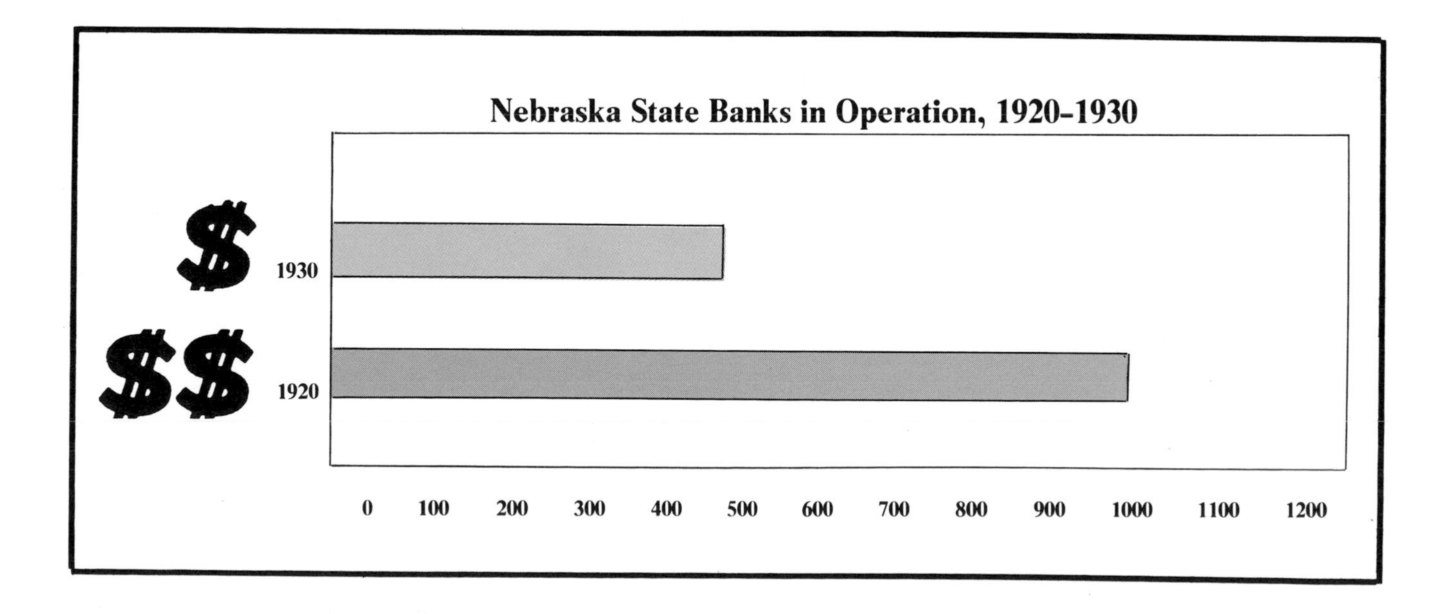
Nebraska State Banks in Operation, 1920-1930
1930
1920
0
100
200
300
400
500
600
700
800
900
1000
1100
1200

The "compounding effect" of change led to bad consequences.

Depression Arrives

Economists, the scientists who study about income and prosperity, invented the word depression (DE-PRES-SION). A depression is a period of time when great numbers of people lose their jobs and cannot find work. It is a period of time when people who owe money cannot pay their debts. As a depression continues, profits from business and farming decrease because people have little money to spend. As profits fall, many businesses go broke. A depression can be a very serious problem for people to solve. There are no easy solutions for bad depressions.

The poor judgments made before and during the 1920's led to a depression in the 1930's. Millions of people in America lost their jobs. Thousands of farmers in America lost their land. Thousands of banks and businesses in America went out of business. The depression of the 1930's was not limited to Nebraska or to the United States. People throughout the world felt the pain brought on by the depression. Like World War I, the depression of the 1930's proved that the people of the world are one big family. What happens in one place affects the people who live in another place.

Important Ideas to Remember from Road to Hardship

During a period of good times, it is easy to exercise poor judgment which can lead to bad consequences at a later time.

The poor judgments made in agriculture, during and immediately after World War I, led to bad consequences for farmers and ranchers in the 1920's and 1930's.

While Nebraska farmers and ranchers enjoyed less prosperity in the 1920's, there were other signs that Nebraska was a prosperous place. Many automobiles were purchased, roads were built, telephones became a common sight in many households, talking movies became popular, and the use of radio swept across the state.

One of the most important projects that began in the 1920's, to be completed in 1932, was the construction of the new Nebraska capitol.

One important idea about change in the age of modern science is that one change can interact with other changes. Usually this happens at a rapid rate and makes the solution of problems more difficult or complex. This idea is called the "compounding effect" of change.

A depression is a period of time when there are few jobs, much unemployment, and people are unable to repay debt.

The poor judgments, made before and during the 1920's, led to a terrible depression in the 1930's.

The depression of the 1930's once again proved that all people in the world are closely tied together in the age of modern science. What happens in one place on the globe affects people in other places in the world.

Things to Do

1. There is no depression at your local library. The only debt you owe is to yourself. You can be paid with high interest by following these guide words.

   MOTION PICTURES
   TELEPHONE
   ELECTRICITY
   RADIO
   NEBRASKA STATE CAPITOL
   ROARING TWENTIES
   PROHIBITION
   FLAPPER
   AGRICULTURE
   THE GREAT DEPRESSION

2. Agriculture is a way of life and a business. Agriculture has been important to Nebraskans from the time of the Woodland people to the present day. You know that science has changed agriculture. You know that agriculture in Nebraska is affected by what happens in other places in the world. Take some time to explore agriculture further.

   In your community you can find people who have some association with agriculture. Your class can brainstorm and make a list of such people. Here are a few questions to consider in making your list. Are there some farmers or ranchers who live nearby? Is there a local banker in your area? Is there a veterinarian who treats farm animals who might live nearby? How about a grain elevator operator? Can you find such an individual in your area? Does your area or community have a seed supplier? What about lawyers in your area who might work with business that pertains to agriculture? Local newspaper people often know a great deal about agriculture. Is there such a person in your area?

   After you have made your list of local experts, invite one or more of these people to your classroom for a discussion. They may have different points of view and different ideas about agriculture. Have a list of questions put together that you want them to address. Again, you can use a class brainstorming session for writing your questions. You may want to ask them questions like the following:

   What do you think are the greatest problems in agriculture today?

   What are some ways that people in agriculture can deal with those problems?

   In what ways do you see agriculture changing in the future?

   What may be some of the good and bad consequences of the changes you see happening in agriculture?

   Good luck in this exploration. It will be fun.

CHAPTER NINETEEN
HARD TIMES

Similar Changes

"The more things change, the more they are the same." Have you ever heard that old saying? Although it sounds funny, there is some truth to it. Change does build upon itself. Over time, change does happen more quickly. Some changes interact with other changes. You know all of those ideas about change. But, how can things change and yet be the same?

In order to answer that question, you need the gift of time. Since history is the story of people's past, it can help you to look back over time. As you look back over time through history, you will make an interesting discovery. Maybe you have already made this discovery in reading *Changing Nebraska*. There are changes that happen in one period of time which are similar to changes that happen in another period of time. Think about some changes you have read about so far. If you think about the horse, you know that the coming of the horse changed life for the native people. The Horse and Buffalo Culture would not have been possible without the horse. So, too, the coming of the automobile changed life for the people of Nebraska in the twentieth century. These two changes happened in different times and with different cultures. Yet, they are similar in some ways. Both changes involved transportation. Both changes resulted in people having greater mobility. Both changes brought about a new life style for people.

The 1930's brought years of great change for Nebraskans. The people who lived during those years believe that period of time to be unique (U-NIQUE), a word that means one of a kind. Through history though, we can see that the changes of the 1930's were like those of earlier times. The more things change, the more they are the same!

Creative Problem Solvers

The decade of the 1930's was a period of years during which Nebraskans faced problems brought about by change. The 1930's was also a period during which Nebraskans dealt with their problems in new and creative ways. There you have the way in which the 1930's were alike and different from other periods in Nebraska's history. Through the gift of time, history allows us to see that change will always bring new problems or challenges. History also shows that Nebraskans are wonderfully creative people. In every age, they deal with the new challenges brought by change in unique ways. Part of your heritage as a Nebraskan is that of creative problem solving.

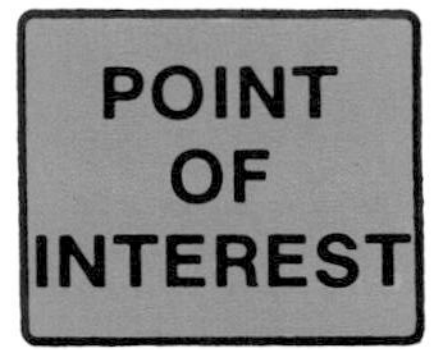

Take some class time for making a list of problems Nebraskans have solved in creative ways. For example, all human beings need shelter. Nebraskans, living in an area with limited timber, have used the earth to build shelters. The native people built earth lodges and the dream chasers built sod houses. Once your list is finished, you will have good evidence to show how Nebraskans have been creative problem solvers over the years.

Now make a new list. Decide what you think are some important problems Nebraskans must solve now or in the future. After the class has agreed upon a list of problems that must be solved, everybody needs to pick a partner. You and your partner are to select one problem from the "to be solved" list. The class can agree upon a working time limit. Within that time limit, no less than one week, each working partnership must uncover all the information they can about the problem they selected. Partners will need time to meet, share information, brainstorm possible solutions, and to create a response. Your only limitation will be your own imagination. Solutions can be in any form. Inventions, drawings, essays, and whatever else the partners agree upon are acceptable.

After the class has shared their creative solutions, your work is not complete. Good ideas need to be shared with others. Some of the best ideas for solving problems have come from people who were willing to share their ideas with people who could act upon those ideas. Is there an idea or solution to a problem that you feel needs to be shared? If so, who should know about the idea and how will you share it? Maybe it's an idea you want to share with a local official like the mayor. If so, how will you share the idea? Will you write to the mayor? Will you invite the mayor into your classroom to discuss the problem and your creative solution? You be the judge. Talk it over with your teacher. Remember, Nebraskans have a long history of being creative problem solvers.

Problems Brought by Change

In agriculture, the problems of the 1920's carried over into the 1930's. Prices for farm goods continued to fall. Farmers sold wheat for $1.00 per bushel in 1929. By 1932, wheat prices stood at .27 per bushel. Corn went from .67 per bushel in 1929 to .13 per bushel in 1932. Oats fell from .38 per bushel in 1929 to .10 per bushel in 1932. Prices farmers received for chickens, eggs, cattle, and hogs all tumbled in the early 1930's.

Farmers not only faced low prices and heavy debt, but nature, as it had done in past history, suddenly caused new problems. Beginning in 1930, the state received less than normal rainfall. During 1934 and 1936, Nebraska received about one-half the rain that normally falls during the course of a year. Summer temperatures soared and crops died in the fields due to heat and lack of moisture. During the spring of 1934, strong winds began blowing across Nebraska and neighboring plains states. The lack of moisture, the dry soil, the poor crops, and the strong winds meant huge dust storms. These terrible dust storms, which could last for days, would darken the day-time skies with dust clouds. Dust blew into houses, caused health problems, and generally got into everything.

Photograph courtesy of the Nebraska State Historical Society

The midday storm approaching Alma darkened the sky.

Photograph courtesy of the Nebraska State Historical Society

The crops able to survive lack of moisture and severe heat were often eaten by grasshoppers.

Dust storms in Nebraska continued off and on throughout the 1930's. By the mid-30's, grasshoppers invaded Nebraska by the millions. Like the farmers of the 1870's, Nebraska farmers in the 1930's battled grasshoppers, heat, and drought. The more things change, the more they are the same.

Problems on the farm were great, but people in towns and cities suffered as well. The number of workers employed by Nebraska manufacturers fell from 29,129 in 1929 to 22,449 in 1939. There were few jobs to be found in towns and cities for people who needed work. People who had work found that their wages were cut. Businesses could not afford to pay high wages. Depression had made life difficult for all people in Nebraska.

Creative Solutions

The first thing the people of Nebraska did during the depression years was to rely upon one another. Those who had work and food were willing to share their small prosperity with those in need. The people in towns and cities set up food kitchens. These were places where people without food and shelter could come to eat and sleep. Church groups set up committees to give out food and clothing to those in need. People often bartered during the depression. A farmer in need of medical care might give a doctor a chicken or two and receive treatment. People caring and showing concern was an important solution to the bad times brought on by the depression.

The 1930's forced Nebraskans to rediscover a truth long known by the native people. The native people viewed the fruits of nature as gifts from the Great Mystery. The native people were grateful for the gifts of nature, and they used them wisely. After the arrival of the dream chasers, and with the use of science, Nebraskans began to take nature for granted. Fragile land was plowed during World War I to plant crops. The widespread destruction of grass and soil cover left the rich soil of the state exposed to the elements of wind and water. The drought of the 1930's, along with the strong winds, caused the rich soil to blow away. The most precious resource of Nebraska was wasted.

In 1932, Franklin Roosevelt was elected President of the United States. When he took office in 1933, President Roosevelt started many programs to help the people of the United States solve problems created by the bad judgments made in earlier years. The Government of the United States gave farmers in Nebraska money to begin soil conservation (CON-SER-VA-TION) work. In soil conservation (CON-SER-VA-TION), farmers were helped to understand how they could farm without destroying the resource of the soil. Grasses were planted to anchor the soil. Farmers were shown how to use contour plowing. Farmers were encouraged to rotate crops, that is not to grow the same crop in the same field year after year. Growing the same crop can drain the soil of important minerals. Nebraskans thought soil conservation was so important that a law was passed by the Nebraska Legislature which divided the state into soil conservation districts or areas. The farmers and ranchers of Nebraska joined as members of soil conservation districts. As members, they cooperated to protect their land. A creative solution to a problem brought on by not respecting the gifts of nature.

President Roosevelt began other programs to help the people of the United States. The Government of the United States passed laws which gave money to the states. State governments used the money to hire people to do important work. In Nebraska, people were hired to build roads, construct buildings, plant grass and trees, and to do other work which made Nebraska a better place to live. Spending public money to give people jobs to accomplish important work was a new idea. Nebraskans accepted this idea as a creative way to solve difficult problems.

Photograph courtesy of the Nebraska State Historical Society

The price paid in erosion when land is abused.

Photograph courtesy Soil Conservation Service

By plowing according to the lay of the land, erosion can be checked and valuable soil can be saved.

Photograph courtesy Soil Conservation Service

During the 1930's, grass was planted on thousands of acres of land to keep the soil from blowing and washing away. Here a worker plants grass seed as part of a soil conservation effort.

During the 1930's, Nebraskans did some things in solving problems that made Nebraska different from other states. In 1934, the people of Nebraska voted to create a unicameral (U-NI-CAM-ER-AL) legislature. In all other states the legislature is divided into two parts or two houses. One house is usually called the "house," and the other house is usually called the "senate." Laws are made when a bill receives the approval of both houses. In Nebraska, the unicameral (U-NI-CAM-ER-AL) is a one-house legislature. Legislators in Nebraska are called "senators." Nebraska is divided up into 49 legislative districts or areas, and there is one senator elected from each district. Nebraska is the only state to have a unicameral legislature. The depression brought hard times, and Nebraskans believed a unicameral legislature would be a more efficient way to do government business. The unicameral legislature now meets every year.

Nebraskans solved another important problem in a creative way during the depression years. Science had given knowledge for the use of electric power. With the invention of electric lights, radio, and modern appliances, people wanted to have electric power brought to their homes. A smart business person could start a company to generate electric power, usually by using water (hydro) or by burning a fossil fuel like coal. Power lines were strung from the power plant to homes and businesses. It was much easier to have electric power in towns and cities where there were many people who lived in one area. For farmers and ranchers, who lived in the open country, getting electric power brought to their homes was expensive if not impossible.

This large electric power plant near Sutherland burns tons of coal everyday to generate electric power used by Nebraskans across the state.

In 1933, the Nebraska Legislature passed a law which allowed the people of the state to form power districts. These were geographic areas where the people could build and operate their own electric power plants. In this manner, it was easier to bring electric power to all the people of the state at the cheapest price. This idea is called "public power." By the mid-1940's, all Nebraskans were served by public power. Nebraska is the only state where the people receive all their electric power through public power districts. In other states, people still buy some or all their electric power from private companies. Public power has worked well in Nebraska and remains a creative solution to a difficult problem.

Hard Times – Good Times

The 1930's were tough years—low prices for farm products, drought, heat, thousands of people without work, food, or shelter. These were some of the most difficult years for the people of Nebraska. During the decade of the 1930's, 65,000 people left the state seeking a better life elsewhere. Although Nebraska lost population, Nebraskans made important gains. There was a rediscovery of our heritage. Nebraskans are people of the earth, and they discovered once again that the earth must be treated with loving care.

Nebraskans gained a renewed sense of the importance of family and friends. As always, during difficult times, people turn towards family and friends for understanding and the sharing of simple pleasures. Nebraskans also gained a greater sense of caring for their fellow human beings. Many people were in need, and efforts were made to help those with the greatest needs.

Perhaps most important, Nebraskans gained greater confidence in themselves. They took bold steps in solving problems with creative ideas. Maybe the hard times of the 1930's were really good times. What do you think?

Important Ideas to Remember from Hard Times

Changes that happen in one period of time are sometimes similar to changes that happen in another period of time.

History is the story of our past. Through history, we can look at the past over time and see how important changes in one period can be similar to changes in another period.

The people of Nebraska have a long history of being creative problem solvers. The people of Nebraska have sometimes found unique solutions to difficult problems.

The 1930's was a decade of depression which presented many difficult problems to the people of of Nebraska.

During the 1930's, the farmers and ranchers of Nebraska faced the problems of low prices for their products, drought, severe heat, grasshoppers, and terrible dust storms which blew away rich soil.

During the 1930's, the people living in the towns and cities of Nebraska faced the problems of low income, no jobs, and the need for food, shelter, and clothing.

The people of Nebraska found one creative solution to the problems of the 1930's in the way they treated one another. People in Nebraska shared their limited wealth and showed concern for the less fortunate.

Under the leadership of President Franklin Roosevelt, the Government of the United States made money available to the people of Nebraska to help solve the problems of the 1930's.

Nebraskans used federal money to start programs in soil conservation, to provide jobs for people needing work, and to make improvements in the state so people could lead better lives.

Nebraskans were willing to try other solutions to solve difficult problems. Nebraskans agreed to set up a one-house legislature called a unicameral. Nebraska remains the only state in the Union with a unicameral legislature. Nebraskans also set up a system of public power. Nebraska is the only state in the Union where the people receive all electric power from public power sources. The people in other states buy some or all of their power from private power companies.

During the 1930's, Nebraskans found that they could rely upon family, friends, neighbors, and other Nebraskans to solve the problems they held in common.

Things to Do

1. You will not have hard times in following these guide words. They can lead you to valuable information about creative problem solving.

   GREAT DEPRESSION
   NEW DEAL
   FRANKLIN DELANO ROOSEVELT
   SOIL CONSERVATION SERVICE
   DUST BOWL
   SHELTER BELT
   NEBRASKA UNICAMERAL
   NEBRASKA PUBLIC POWER
   GEORGE NORRIS

2. There are several important lessons that come to us from the great depression of the 1930's. Nebraskans learned that being wasteful has bad consequences. Nebraskans learned that people are responsible for the resources given to them through nature. Nebraskans learned that they have responsibility for their fellow human beings. Nebraskans learned that problems which seem hard to solve can be solved if people cooperate and work together. These are lessons that can be too easily forgotten. The world will never be a perfect place. It is easy to complain about the bad things we see in life. What Nebraskans did to solve their problems in the 1930's is an example for all of us.

   Bring back the spirit of the thirties in your classroom and community. What can you and your class do to reach out to others? What can you and your class do to encourage the wise use of resources? Are there ways in which you can promote cooperation to solve some problems?

Personal note from the author—As you think about the questions above, let me describe for you a project that I will always remember from my school days. Every year at the elementary school I attended we had a newspaper collection drive. Kids worked together to gather as many newspapers as possible. We brought the papers to the school grounds on an agreed upon day, and we all helped to bundle them for pick up by a truck. We sold the papers and gave the money earned to charity. That one project allowed all of the kids in the school to work together. It allowed us to recycle a resource and helped to save a few trees. It allowed us to reach out to other people in need and to give them some help. It was not an earth shaking activity that changed the world forever. It was an activity that helped us make a statement. We were able to say to the world: "We care and we can make a difference." I think that is the spirit of the thirties.

3. Within your own community you can find people who lived during the great depression years of the 1930's. Maybe your parents or teacher can help identify such a person or persons. If so, offer an invitation to visit your classroom. You might ask that your visitor bring photographs, phonographic records, newspapers, and other materials from the 1930's. Be prepared to look, listen, and ask lots of questions. This will be your chance to take a trip into the past. Do not miss it!

CHAPTER TWENTY
WORLD WAR II

When Will We Learn?

Drums, the distant drums.
They beat out WAR. WAR.
Not again. Not again.
When will we ever learn?

The 1930's found Nebraskans wrapped up in the problems of the depression. Little attention was given to events in Europe and Asia. Many Nebraskans, like other Americans, had forgotten the great change brought by World War I. Events in faraway places affect all people. Things did happen in the 1920's and 30's which led to another world war.

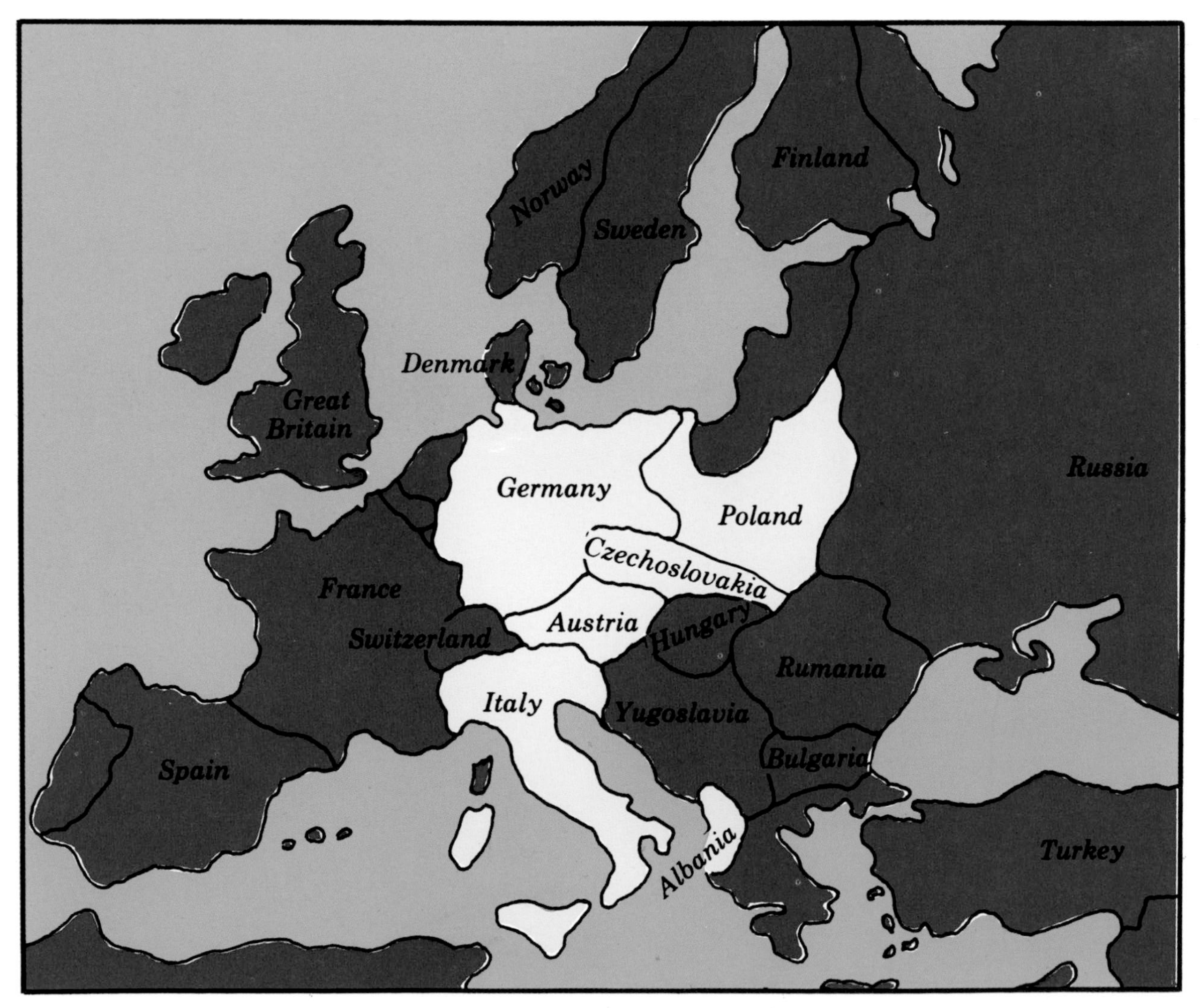

Hitler used the powerful armed forces of Germany to invade countries in Europe during the 1930's and 1940's.

The Allies and Central Powers had signed a treaty to end World War I. According to the treaty, Germany had to admit blame for World War I. Germany was made to disarm, and the German people were forced to pay a large sum of money to the Allies for damages done during the war. Some German people blamed the treaty for problems Germany suffered after the war. There were shortages of food and other goods. Many people could not find work. The problems of Germany were made worse by the world-wide depression of the 1930's.

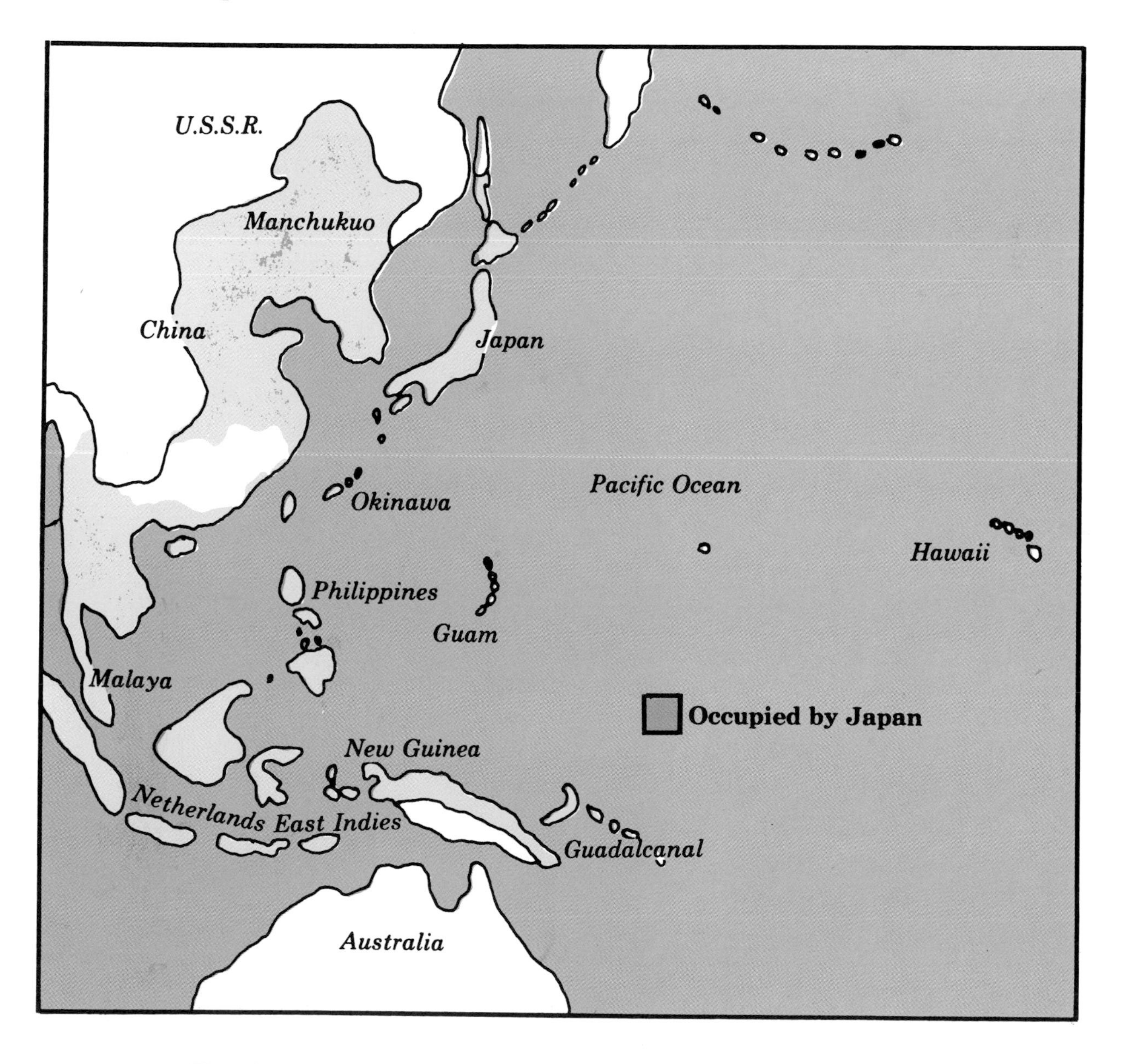

The Japanese military forces enlarged the Empire of Japan by invading countries of Asia and the Pacific Ocean area.

From these terrible conditions a man named Adolf Hitler got control of the German Government. Hitler started a group called the Nazis. Hitler and his Nazi followers said Germany would no longer obey the agreements of the treaty that ended World War I. The Nazis gave people jobs making weapons of war. Hitler organized a large army and expanded Germany's borders by moving into neighboring countries (see map).

While Hitler and the Nazis moved Europe closer to war, events in Asia and the Pacific were also going badly. Japan was a country of growing strength. People who believed in great military power took control of the Japanese Government in the early 1930's. The Japanese, like the Germans, wanted to expand their power over other countries. They used their army, navy, and air force to take new land.

In September, 1939, war broke out in Europe. At first England and France fought Germany. The Germans defeated France in June, 1940, and England stood alone against Hitler and the German war machine. Many Nebraskans were worried, and they wanted the United States to stay out of this new war. Although the United States did not get involved at first, the Government of the United States gave some help to the people of England. On December 7, 1941, the Japanese bombed the American naval fleet at Pearl Harbor, Hawaii. Eighteen American ships were sunk and over 3,700 Americans were killed or wounded. The attack on Pearl Harbor brought the United States into the war against Japan and Germany. The countries of Germany, Italy, and Japan (known as the Axis Powers) fought against the countries of the United States, England, and Russia (known as the Allies).

World War II was fought on the continents of Africa, Asia, and Europe, and on the Atlantic and Pacific Oceans. The war ended in 1945. It was the most terrible war ever fought. More people were killed, more property was destroyed, and more money was spent on death and destruction than ever before. Over 16,000,000 people were killed in the war at a cost of more than $1,150,000,000,000. Once again, the leaders of important countries chose to use knowledge gained from science in developing horrible weapons. The United States brought the war to an end when American bombers dropped atomic bombs on the Japanese cities of Hiroshima and Nagasaki in August, 1945. At Hiroshima more than 92,000 people were killed by one bomb. Another 40,000 people were killed by the bomb dropped on Nagasaki.

Photograph courtesy The Bettman Archives, Inc.

The Japanese air attack on the American naval fleet in Pearl Harbor, Hawaii, brought the United States into World War II.

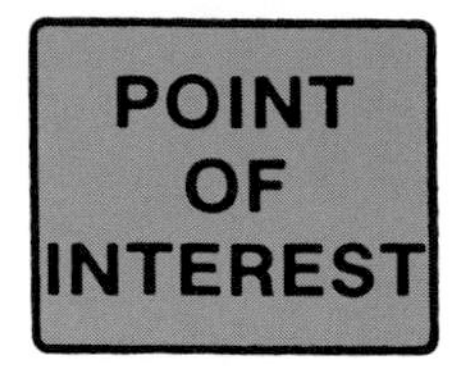

Beliefs and Actions

Personal note from the author—The invention of atomic weapons brought a most dangerous change to warfare. Since the end of World War II, several countries have made atomic weapons. The United States and Russia have the greatest number of weapons. A war between the United States and Russia could mean the end of life on earth! People must put an end to war before war puts an end to people. How can war be stopped? How can you, a single individual, help bring an end to war? One way every person can join in an effort to end war is by making a list of beliefs and actions. In this manner, you can state what you believe and what you can do to act on those beliefs. The following is a list of beliefs and actions that I have drawn up for myself. What do you believe and what can you do to end war?

BELIEF

I believe that ignorance has been a cause of war.

ACTIONS

1. I will read history to get a better understanding of what has happened in the past and what can happen in the future.
2. I will read books, newspapers, and magazines to understand what is happening in the present and what may happen in the future.
3. I will learn all I can every day. Learning does not begin and end in school!

BELIEF

I believe that people are smart enough to end war.

ACTIONS

1. I will not accept the attitude of those who say: "There have always been wars and war will always be with us."
2. Elected officials in the United States, including all officials in Nebraska, work for the citizens. I will write and talk to my elected officials. I want them to constantly hear the message that we must have peace in the world. Elected officials must work harder for peace.

BELIEF

I believe world peace begins with a state of mind.

ACTIONS

1. I will work hard to eliminate pettiness, bitterness, and hatred within myself.
2. I will work hard to treat all people with respect.
3. I will not judge the worth of another human being by his/her race, sex, age, or beliefs.

One last word—In reading the story of *Changing Nebraska*, I hope you have discovered that people are capable of planning for the future. Through careful planning and hard work, people can shape their future. People can cause good changes to happen in the future. In the 1930's, Nebraskans learned from past mistakes. They saw what happened when they did not take care of the soil. Efforts in soil conservation came about because people decided it was time for a change. The same holds true for today. We must plan and then work hard to bring an end to war. You and I can make this change happen. First we must believe and then we must act!

Nebraskans at War

The bombing of Pearl Harbor shocked most Nebraskans. Suddenly, the country was at war. As in World War I, Nebraskans supported the war effort by buying bonds. Like other Americans, Nebraskans were called upon to make sacrifices. The Government of the United States declared that the most important business for all Americans was to win the war. A plan was set up to ration (RA-TION) important resources. In rationing, people were given coupons and stamps. People could buy a limited amount of goods each month by using their coupons and stamps. The government rationed food, gasoline, shoes, automobile tires, and many other goods. In this way, most resources were used to produce goods for the armed forces.

During World War II, the use of airplanes was very important. Huge bombers carried tons of bombs which were dropped on targets in Europe and Asia. A large factory opened near Omaha was called the Martin Bomber Plant. Thousands of Nebraskans were hired to build bombers that were used against Germany and Japan. The "Enola Gay," the B-29 bomber that dropped the atomic bomb on Hiroshima, was built near Omaha.

The Army Air Force established air bases across Nebraska during World War II. The prairies of Nebraska proved to be an excellent place to train air crews for combat. Air bases were opened near Alliance, Ainsworth, Bruning, Fairmont, Grand Island, Harvard, Kearney, Lincoln, McCook, Scottsbluff, and Scribner. Nebraskans also had a hand in making bombs and shells used in the war. Large plants were opened near Grand Island, Mead, and Sidney where people worked making explosives. In addition, the U.S. Navy opened a large ammunition depot to store explosives near Hastings.

The most important contribution made by Nebraskans in the war effort was the production of food. Just as in World War I, Nebraska farmers and ranchers were asked to grow and produce large amounts of food. Nature was ready to cooperate in helping farmers and ranchers produce food. Nebraska began receiving more normal rainfall again by 1941. The drought of the 1930's was over. Prices soared along with crop and animal production. Prosperity had returned to Nebraska.

Benefits and Losses

World War II saw the end of the depression. Farmers and ranchers received record high prices for their produce. New businesses were opened to manufacture products used in fighting the war. There were jobs for all who wanted work. Of course, the price for all this prosperity was high. Over 120,000 Nebraska men and women served in the armed forces of the United States during World War II. A total of 3,839 Nebraskans lost their lives in the war. Thousands of others were wounded and injured. Once again, Nebraskans learned that they are citizens of the world. What happens in faraway places does affect the people of Nebraska.

Photograph courtesy The Bettman Archives, Inc.

The use of the atomic bomb destroyed the city of Hiroshima, Japan, and brought a quick end to World War II.

Important Ideas to Remember from World War II

Like many other Americans, most Nebraskans were caught up in the depression and ignored what was happening in Europe and Asia during the 1930's.

In Europe, Adolf Hitler had taken control of the government.

Hitler refused to obey the agreements in the treaty that ended World War I. He built up the German military and invaded other countries in Europe.

In Japan, persons believing in the use of military power to expand into other countries had taken control of the government.

Japanese military forces were used to expand the territory of the Empire of Japan.

In September, 1939, war broke out in Europe.

Most Nebraskans wanted the United States to stay out of the new war.

On December 7, 1941, Japanese airplanes bombed the American naval fleet in Pearl Harbor, Hawaii, and the United States entered into World War II.

In World War II, the countries of Germany, Japan, and Italy were known as the Axis Powers. The Axis Powers fought against the countries of the United States, England, and Russia who were known as the Allies.

Nebraskans made many contributions to help the Allies win the war. Some of the important contributions made by Nebraskans included buying war bonds, rationing resources, and building airplanes and explosives.

One of the most important ways Nebraskans contributed to the war effort was by producing food for the Allies.

Nebraskans also gave their lives in the effort to defeat the Axis Powers. Over 120,000 Nebraskans served in the armed forces of the United States during World War II. Nearly 4,000 Nebraskans died in fighting the Axis Powers.

World War II brought an end to the depression in Nebraska and across the United States.

Things to Do

1. Read for peace. Develop a better understanding of the world by following these guide words:

   AXIS POWERS
   NAZIISM
   FASCISM

DEMOCRACY
ADOLF HITLER
BENITO MUSSOLINI
PEARL HARBOR
ATOMIC BOMB
NUCLEAR WEAPONS
HIROSHIMA
NAGASAKI
WINSTON CHURCHILL
FRANKLIN DELANO ROOSEVELT
JOSEPH STALIN
UNITED NATIONS

2. During any period of war, there is music written and sung that expresses the feelings, the hopes, and the joy of a people. World War II was no exception. It was a period of time known as the "Big Band Era." Many large bands provided entertainment for the fighting troops. Usually these bands had vocalists who sang the songs the men and women in uniform wanted to hear. If you have a music teacher in your school, ask that person to help find some of the music and songs that were popular in World War II. If your school does not have a music teacher, ask your classroom teacher to help. You might find a person in your community who has kept music and records from the World War II era. Fortunately, many of the World War II songs were preserved on records, just the way they were performed by the bands and vocalists of the period.

   Rather than simply listening to the music, put on a performance. Find some photographs of how people dressed during that period. You can enlist the help of your parents, grandparents, teachers, and other interested citizens to sponsor a World War II performance.

   One thing that happened during the war was the establishment of United Service Organizations clubs. These were places where soldiers and sailors went to be entertained. Since there were so many young men in the armed forces, they would frequently go to USO clubs to listen to the music, dance with young women volunteers, and eat some home-cooked food. You might want to make your classroom into a USO club for an evening. Be sure to invite some World War II veterans to your club. They would enjoy hearing the music and remembering old times. They might have some stories to share with you. Good luck and have fun.

CHAPTER TWENTY-ONE
THE NEW AGE—PART I

The Turning Point

Have you ever heard the phrase "turning point?" Sometimes people use that phrase in talking about important times in their lives. A person might refer to a particular event as being so important that it changed his/her life forever. In such a case, the event and when the event happened becomes a turning point. World War II was a turning point in modern history. The events of the war have gone a long way in shaping how people live today. The end of the war marks the beginning of a new age. It is an age of growing knowledge and prosperity. It is an age of technology and bigness. It is an age of great change. Like other ages in Nebraska's history, it offers promise and problems.

New Prosperity

World War II brought an end to the depresssion. Farm prices and farm production reached new heights. Jobs were plentiful, but goods to buy had been rationed during the war. When the war ended, Americans were ready to use money saved during the war to buy new products. Farmers wanted new machinery to work their farms. Millions of Americans were ready to buy new cars. No new cars had been made during the war. Men and women leaving the armed forces had saved money during the war. They were ready to spend money on things they had not been able to get during the war. Businesses that manufactured war goods quickly began to make products the American people wanted to buy.

This new prosperity is one of the greatest changes brought by the war. Growing knowledge gained through science has continued to make new goods and services available to the American people. Not all groups or individuals in the United States have shared in the new prosperity, but Americans have not known widespread depression since the 1930's.

Prosperity in Nebraska Agriculture

Nebraskans have shared in the new prosperity since the end of World War II. In agriculture, as in other areas of life, new knowledge gained through science brought problems and promise. Study the graph on page 185. The solid line tells you that the number of farms in Nebraska has fallen from under 110,000 in 1950 to under 65,000 in 1980. The dotted line tells you that the average size of a Nebraska farm has grown from 450 acres in 1950 to about 750 acres in 1980. Since the end of World War II, the trend in Nebraska has been towards fewer farms and larger farms. What does this mean and why has this happened?

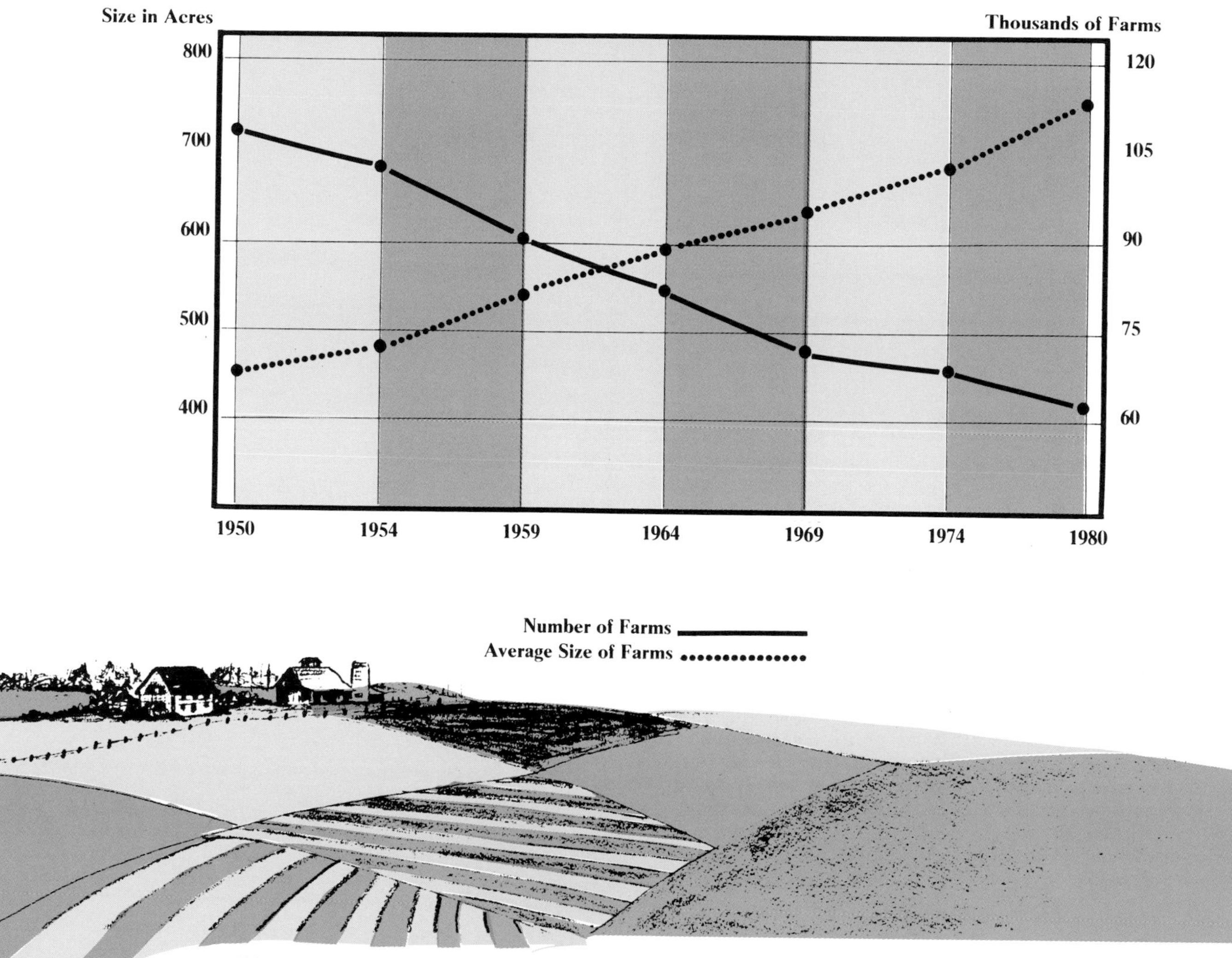

You already know that knowledge gained through science changed farming in Nebraska. New machines, new types of plants, the use of chemicals, efforts in soil conservation, careful selection and breeding of animals, and the coming of electric power were but a few of the forces for change. A single farmer, using the tools and knowledge gained from science, can work more land than ever before. Nebraska farmers have also employed science to bring needed water to their land. The state of Nebraska rests on top of a huge underground water supply. Wells have been drilled and water has been pumped to the surface to use on crop land. A look at the graph on page 186 shows how the use of irrigation in Nebraska has increased. Although water is taken from streams and rivers, most water used in irrigation is pumped from the ground.

Number of Acres Irrigated, 1950/1981
(By Crop Reporting Districts)

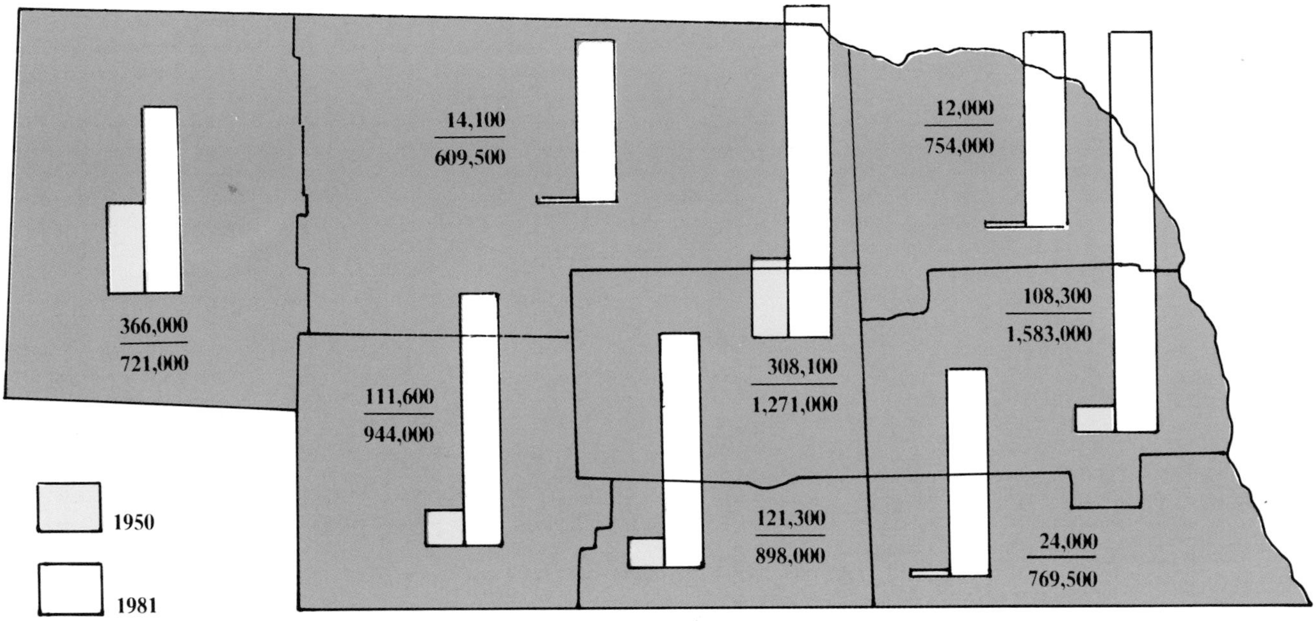

366,000 / 721,000
14,100 / 609,500
111,600 / 944,000
308,100 / 1,271,000
121,300 / 898,000
12,000 / 754,000
108,300 / 1,583,000
24,000 / 769,500
1950
1981

The figures below will tell you what the application of science in agriculture has meant to Nebraskans.

Production in Bushels					
Crop	1940	1950	1960	1970	1980
Corn	95,489,000	241,560,000	333,438,000	367,275,000	603,500,000
Wheat	34,725,000	88,842,000	85,712,000	97,204,000	108,300,000
Beans	56,000	1,200,000	4,592,000	17,864,000	53,100,000

Can you see a problem for Nebraska farmers in the information provided by the graphs and charts? There are fewer farmers operating larger farms and growing more crops. If you think there might be a problem, take a piece of paper and write down what you think the problem might be for Nebraska farmers.

You and your classmates have probably been able to identify several problems faced by Nebraska farmers. One problem deals with overproduction. Do you remember what happened after World War I? Nebraska farmers increased their production during the war. When the war ended, production stayed high but prices fell because there was too much food. Farmers have faced the same problem since the end of World War II. Many small farmers have been unable to stay in business. It costs a great deal of money to buy equipment, fertilizer, seed, fuel, and other things needed to run a farm. Farmers usually borrow money from banks to buy what they need to raise crops and animals. If prices for farm products are low, farmers cannot pay their debts. Farmers must either get more land to raise more crops or sell their land to other farmers who operate larger farms. A small farmer who buys more land must usually borrow money to buy the land. When this happens, the farmer goes deeper into debt and must hope that increased production will help pay the debt. If prices are too low, the farmer cannot pay the debt and is forced to sell farm land to pay the debt.

The problem of overproduction in Nebraska agriculture is difficult to solve. Farmers have used knowledge gained through science to produce too much food. Prices for food goods have remained low. The result is fewer farmers with larger farms. In order to be successful, farmers have to plan carefully. Successful farmers and ranchers often use computers to help them plan. Farming is not the same business it was when the dream chasers came to Nebraska. Although modern farmers still contend with weather and insects, successful farmers must be able to work with their minds as well as with their hands. In the new age since World War II, education and knowledge have become the keys to prosperity in agriculture.

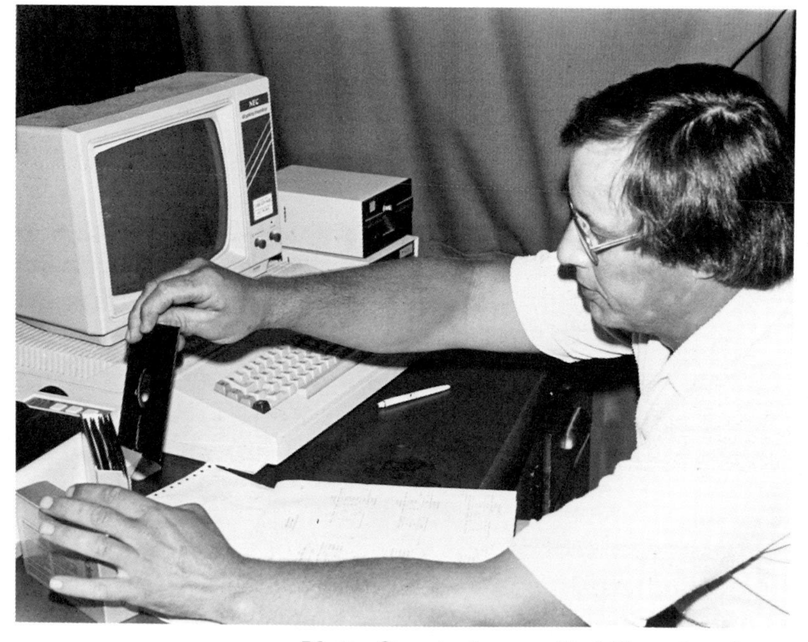

Platte County farmer Rod Hassebrook
photo by Dave Howe, courtesy of "Nebraska Farmer"

Using computer technology in agriculture has become necessary in the new age.

Prosperity in Nebraska Towns and Cities

When scientists talk about population, they often use the terms "rural" and "urban." For most of its history, Nebraska has been a rural state. That means that the majority of the people lived on farms, ranches, and in small towns. In the new age, Nebraska has become an urban state where the majority of people live in larger towns and cities.

Study the chart below and you can see what has happened to Nebraska's population since the beginning of the new age.

Year	Population	Urban	Rural
1940	1,315,834	39%	61%
1950	1,315,510	47%	53%
1960	1,411,921	54%	46%
1970	1,485,333	61%	39%
1980	1,569,825	63%	37%

POINT OF INTEREST

Graphically Speaking

How could you show the above figures on a graph? Pick a partner. You and your partner decide what kind of graph would best show how Nebraska's population has changed from rural to urban since the beginning of the new age. What would work best? Would a line graph, a pie graph, or a bar graph give a reader the most information in the shortest time? Or is there another way to show graphically what has happened to Nebraska's population? Once your partner and you decide how it's to be done, set up a scale, draw the graph, and color it.

When the graph-making activity is finished, hang your creations in the classroom. These are colorful messages that tell you something important about Nebraska's population. They show an important change in how people live in Nebraska. The graphs are also a reminder. Important information of all kinds is communicated through graphs. Keep your eyes open for the use of graphs in newspapers, magazines, and on television. Some scientists say that the United States has become a visual society. What does that mean? Why would the use of graphs be important in a visual society?

You already know that there are fewer farmers operating larger farms in modern Nebraska. Another trend that you can see from the chart and your graph is that people in Nebraska have moved from farms and small towns to cities and larger towns. The move from rural to urban in Nebraska means that people are more likely to find work in urban areas. Why do you think that is true?

There has been a growth of jobs in urban areas. Many jobs in urban areas are related to agriculture. People are employed to prepare or manufacture food products. Can you think of a food product made in Nebraska that you eat or that is used to feed animals?

With more people living in urban areas, there is greater need for services. People need to use services provided by doctors, lawyers, banks, restaurants, repair shops, health clubs, schools, and many other service providers. Large numbers of people are employed in providing services to others. Service jobs are one of the fastest growing areas of employment in urban Nebraska.

The growth of service jobs shows that Nebraskans are enjoying greater prosperity. It costs money to use the services of a doctor or to eat in a restaurant. Economists often measure prosperity by adding up the amount of money people earn in a year. Economists have found that in 1980 the people of Nebraska earned about 25 times the amount of money they earned in 1940!

Photograph courtesy of Omaha Chamber of Commerce

Urban Nebraska has grown in the new age. The growth in prosperity has allowed people in urban areas to seek many services in large centers.

Despite the growth of prosperity and promise in urban Nebraska, there are problems that Nebraskans must solve. Some people in urban Nebraska are unable to find work and live in poverty. In the cities of Omaha and Lincoln, increased automobile traffic means more traffic accidents and greater air pollution. Crime rates tend to be higher in urban areas, and people are seeking more ways to prevent crime. As is true in the rural areas, the people of urban Nebraska have found that knowledge and education are the keys to building a better tomorrow.

Prosperity and Promise

Growing prosperity in Nebraska is a change that has led to other changes (the multiplier effect). The growing prosperity has affected where people live and how they earn a living. In a prosperous Nebraska, people want more and better services. Sometimes government has been called upon to provide those services. In Nebraska, state and local government has grown in size because people ask for more services.

Growing prosperity has also forced Nebraskans to think hard about how to make certain all people share in the prosperity of the new age. Some groups and individuals in Nebraska have not been treated fairly over the years. The Nebraska state motto, "Equality Before the Law," is a promise made to all citizens. When some people are not treated as equally as others because of race, sex, age or beliefs, it is a problem that must be solved.

Important Ideas to Remember from the New Age

A turning point is an important moment in history which marks the end of one age and the beginning of a new age.

World War II was a turning point in modern history.

In Nebraska, World War II marked the end of the depression period and the beginning of a new age of prosperity.

The new age of prosperity in Nebraska has seen a decline in the number of farms, but a growth in the size of farms.

The new age in Nebraska has seen a shift in where people live.

Nebraska has gone from a rural state to an urban state during the new age.

The new age in Nebraska has resulted in a great growth in services.

More people are employed in providing services and more people are using services.

During the new age in Nebraska, people have had a greater need for education and knowledge.

A great challenge of the new age in Nebraska is to make certain that all people are given equal opportunity to share in the new prosperity.

Things to Do

1. Guide words to lead you to a new age of prosperity.

   RURAL
   URBAN
   SUBURBAN
   OGALLALA AQUIFER
   IRRIGATION
   GROUND WATER
   SURFACE WATER
   FUTURE JOBS
   EQUAL OPPORTUNITY

2. One of the guide words found in this chapter is "future jobs." Take some time to do some reading about future jobs. The new age is a period of rapid change. Jobs exist today that were not dreamed of a few years ago. Some jobs that were once very important in Nebraska and other places have disappeared. Futurists (scientists who study about what is possible and probable in the future) predict that people in the future will change jobs more frequently. This means that during your life you will have greater need for knowledge and education in order to do different jobs.

   If this is true, think about the future. Your assignment is to write a story about yourself and your classmates. The time is fifty years in the future. Describe where you are living and what job you are doing. Use your imagination in writing this story. You might even describe how your children, or those of your classmates, are being educated. Do they have schools fifty years in the future? Do you have robots that help you do your work? How do people get around? Do people still use automobiles? If so, how are they powered? Do most people still live in urban areas? Are farmers still having problems with overproduction?

   When you and your classmates have completed your essays, share them with others. You might want to use the essays as the basis for writing a play. It would be great fun to produce a play about the future for teachers and parents. Creating a set with all the costuming and props would be a big job, but it might prove to be exciting and fun. What do you think?

CHAPTER TWENTY-TWO
THE NEW AGE—PART II

The End of Isolation

The turning point of World War II saw Nebraska change from a rural state to an urban state. The size of Nebraska's farms grew as the inventions and discoveries of science were used, allowing fewer farmers to produce more food than ever before.

Perhaps the greatest change of the new age was the end to isolation (ISO-LA-TION). Isolation means to be set apart. In a sense, Nebraskans have been isolated for much of their history. The native people lived in isolation, apart from the rest of the country, until the time of exploration and settlement. When the dream chasers came to Nebraska, they lived in isolation, apart from families and friends they left in other places. The events of World War I briefly ended isolation for Nebraskans. During the 1920's and 1930's, Nebraskans returned to a life of isolation. Nebraska was still a rural state with poor roads. Most farms had no electricity. The depression years only added to the sense of isolation as Nebraskans worked to solve their problems.

World War II was the turning point that ended isolation for Nebraska. Winning the war required an effort from all Americans. When the war ended, big changes came together to end Nebraska's isolation. Those changes continue to affect your life today. Nebraskans are no longer isolated from one another or from the rest of the world.

World Events

World War II made all Americans understand the idea that events that happen in faraway places affect all people. The war helped to make the United States a world leader. The United States took on new responsibilities in world affairs. One role Americans were forced to accept was that of defender of the free world. The leaders of the United States promised that America would keep a strong military force. The United States would always be ready to respond to an attack by countries which oppose democracy.

In building a system of defense against possible attacks from enemies, the Government of the United States called upon the people of Nebraska to help. In 1948, the United States Air Force established a new command called the Strategic Air Command (SAC). The headquarters for SAC is located at Offutt Air Base near Bellevue. The Strategic Air Command also has nuclear missiles housed in underground silos in western Nebraska. The job of SAC is to defend freedom by having the power to destroy the enemies of democracy. If the United States or its allies were attacked by an enemy, the Strategic Air Command would control aircraft and missiles around the world that could be used in the defense of the United States.

The presence of the Strategic Air Command is a daily reminder to Nebraskans of their involvement in world affairs. The huge underground command center at Offutt Air Base links SAC and Nebraska to the entire world. New information is processed through the command center twenty-four hours a day. The isolation of Nebraska is a thing of the past.

Photograph courtesy of SAC, Offutt Air Force Base

The SAC command center near Bellevue plays an important role in the defense of America in the new age.

Networks

A network is set up when a series of things are connected. For example, your school is wired for electricity. Every socket, switch, and light is connected by a set of wires which eventually connect to a main power source. There is an electrical network in your school.

The idea of networking is of the most importance in the new age. In Nebraska, many networks were established which linked all parts of the state together and which linked Nebraska to the rest of the United States and to the entire world. These networks were made possible by the knowledge gained through science.

One network you are familiar with is television. Just as radio linked Nebraska with the world in the 1920's and 1930's, television came on to the scene in the 1950's. Actually, the first two television stations in Nebraska were established in Omaha during the summer of 1949. During the 1950's, ten more stations were established in Nebraska. More television stations have been added since the 1950's. Most Nebraska television stations are connected to national television networks. Nebraskans also established an educational televison network. Programs are sent across the education network from Lincoln to all parts of the state. You probably watch instructional television in your school. Instructional television programs are broadcast over the educational television network. Your school tunes into the network and uses the programs.

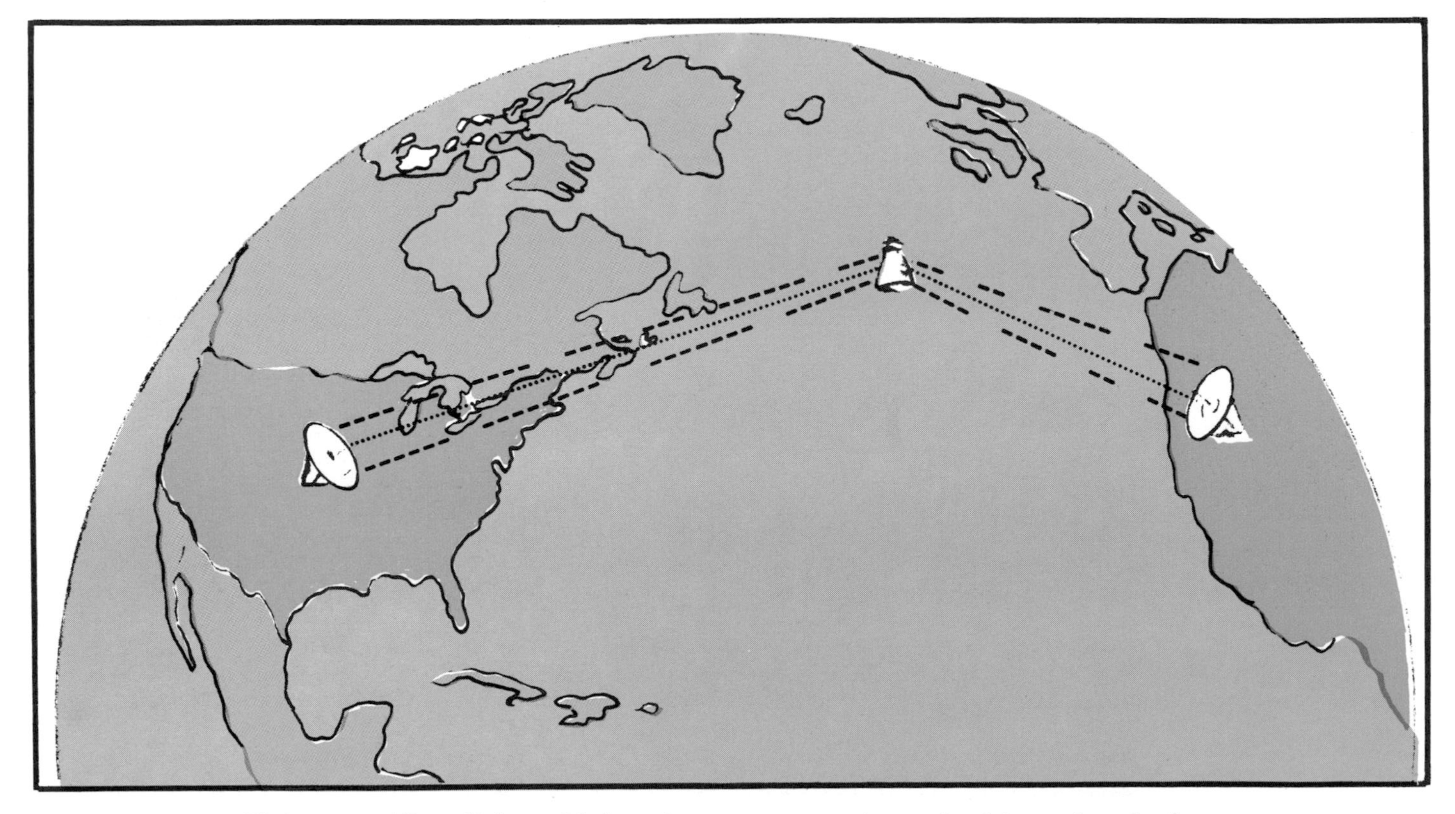

Using satellite dishes, Nebraskans can receive television signals from any place on earth. Isolation is no longer possible for Nebraskans in the new age.

Television has had a powerful effect on Nebraskans. It is now possible for people in Nebraska to see events that happen in any place in the world and beyond. In 1969, when the lunar space craft landed on the moon, Nebraskans sat in their homes and watched the first human beings to walk on the moon. Nebraskans are also able to receive instant television coverage of important events that are happening in Nebraska. Television, more than any other invention of science, has helped to end isolation for Nebraskans.

Important networks for transportation and travel have also been developed in the new age. The end of World War II found Nebraska unprepared for the growth in automobile travel. Nebraska's roads had been neglected during the great depression and the war. In some areas of the state, there were no hard-surfaced roads. With the purchase of many new automobiles following the war, a great demand for a network of good roads was created.

As the roads of Nebraska were repaired and improved upon in the 1940's and 1950's, another important event happened. The Government of the United States wanted to create an interstate highway network that would connect the entire country. A law was passed by the Congress of the United States in 1956. This new law gave large sums of money to every state to participate in the building of the interstate highway network. In June, 1957, construction began on a six-mile stretch of Interstate Highway 80 in Sarpy County. Nebraska had entered the age of interstate highways. Nebraska Interstate Highway 80 was completed in 1974. This great highway is used by thousands of motorists each day, and Interstate 80 links Nebraska to all parts of the United States.

The modern interstate highway in Nebraska helped bring an end to isolation.

As you may remember from Chapter Nine, the need for a transcontinental railroad had much to do with Nebraska becoming a state. The railroads brought thousands of settlers to Nebraska and were the most important networks that linked Nebraska to other parts of the country. Since World War II, railroading in Nebraska began to change rapidly. Railroads continued to carry goods to and from Nebraska, but fewer passengers traveled on trains. Since people in Nebraska were moving from rural to urban areas, the railroads decided to stop providing train service to rural areas. Most small towns in Nebraska are no longer served by railroads. Only two passenger trains were operating in Nebraska by 1985. One eastbound and one westbound train travel along the main route of the Burlington Railroad through Omaha, Lincoln, Hastings, and McCook. The railroads of Nebraska are now used to haul freight or goods used by people. Most freight hauled by Nebraska railroads passes through Nebraska going to other places.

In the new age, speed and convenience are important to people. Airline travel in Nebraska has grown rapidly since the end of World War II. With over one hundred public airports, more than one million passengers fly in and out of Nebraska each year. The jet airliner has replaced the railroad as the largest public transporter of people. Nebraskans can now reach any part of the world in a matter of hours. The inventions of science have brought a swift end to isolation. Nebraskans went from the Horse and Buffalo Culture to the Jet Age in a period of one hundred years!

Photograph courtesy of Omaha Chamber of Commerce

Jet air travel helped to end isolation for Nebraska. Nebraskans can travel to most places in the world in a matter of hours.

Knowledge Explosion

Science, the way of learning that has changed modern life, has increased the amount of knowledge known to human beings at a rapid rate. Some people refer to this growth of knowledge in the new age as the "knowledge explosion." The knowledge explosion means that by using the tools of science, people are gaining new knowledge and making new discoveries every day. The amount of knowledge in the world is growing so fast that the rate of change is constantly speeded up. In such a fast-changing world, education takes on more importance.

When the dream chasers came to Nebraska and set up schools, the main business of schools was to teach youngsters how to read, write, and do arithmetic. A person who mastered those skills was considered to be educated. Do you think schools in Nebraska should teach more than reading, writing, and arithmetic? If so, what else do you need to know or be able to do in the new age?

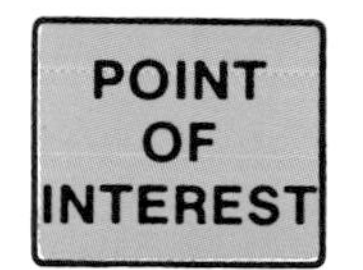

Education in the new age has become more important for Nebraskans. Take time to hold a class discussion. Invite some guests into your classroom to talk about the importance of education in the new age. You might invite your superintendent of schools, your building principal, the president of your school board, or whomever you think might be interested in the topic. Provide your invited guests with a list of questions you want them to respond to during the discussion. The following are some suggested questions you may want to consider to include on your list of questions.

1. Is there a difference between education and schooling? If so, what is the difference?
2. In the past, reading, writing, and arithmetic were considered basic for all educated people. In the new age, are there other things that are basic for an educated person to master? If so, what are those other things?
3. Does the knowledge explosion mean that I might have to go to school forever, or will I be able to learn what I need to know without going to school?

Think up additional questions. Make sure they are questions that help you better understand why education is so important in the new age.

Your Future

The force of change ended the days of isolation for Nebraskans. The people of Nebraska are citizens of a fast-changing world. Networking, the knowledge explosion, and the leadership role of the United States in world affairs has changed life for you and all other Nebraskans.

No one knows for sure what lies ahead in the future. Through reading *Changing Nebraska*, you do know that change has been and will continue to be a force in our lives. There is every reason to believe that there will be more changes in the future. There is every reason to believe that the speed of change will increase in the future. There is every reason to believe that you will have difficult problems to solve in the future. The problem of war has not been solved. Nebraskans have fought in two wars since the end of World War II. There are problems to solve in protecting the environment. Nebraskans have not yet learned to get along as they should.

The future, however, is also full of promise. The knowledge explosion offers new information to help human beings understand more about ourselves and our world. With new knowledge, you have opportunities to make better choices. You can think about consequences before you make choices. For example, people know more about how to live healthy lives in the new age. People have used that knowledge to make choices about what they eat and how they live. The result is that people in Nebraska are living longer than ever before. The same thing holds true in other areas. Choices made with knowledge are usually wiser than choices made in ignorance. Choices made while considering possible consequences are better than choices made with no consideration of the future. The choices you make today go a long way in shaping your future. Through your choices, you can help to direct future change.

The story of *Changing Nebraska* ends and begins with your future. The past is history. You will write the future chapters of *Changing Nebraska* by your actions. You have much to be proud of as a Nebraskan. You have a great heritage to build upon. You have many challenges ahead. How do you want Nebraska to change in the future? You and your classmates will shape the future by your choices.

Photograph courtesy of the Nebraska Department of Economic Development

The future of Nebraska will be determined by your choices. What changes do you want for Nebraska in the future?

Important Ideas to Remember from the New Age

Isolation means to be set apart. For much of Nebraska's history, the people of Nebraska have lived in isolation, apart from others.

The isolation of Nebraska ended with the changes brought by World War II.

One change that ended Nebraska's isolation was the change in world events.

Following World War II, the United States took on the responsibility of protecting democracy in the world.

As the protector of democracy, the United States kept a strong military force. The Strategic Air Command (SAC) was established as an important part of America's new defense efforts.

The Strategic Air Command is headquartered at Offutt Air Base near Bellevue. There are also missile silos in Nebraska under the command of SAC.

The presence of the Strategic Air Command in Nebraska is a constant reminder to Nebraskans that they are part of the world community.

Another important change that ended Nebraska's isolation in the new age was the establishment of several important networks.

Nebraskans saw the establishment of television network connections across the state following World War II.

Television has helped to end isolation in Nebraska by allowing Nebraskans to see events that are happening anywhere in the world as they happen.

A network of paved roads and highways was completed in Nebraska following World War II. Especially important in this network of roads is Interstate Highway 80. Interstate 80 is part of a network that connects Nebraska to all other states in the country. The interstate highway network has done much to end the isolation of Nebraska.

Although railroads are still important networks that link Nebraska to other places, most railroads haul freight through Nebraska in the new age.

Networks established by the use of jet airliners link Nebraskans to all parts of the world.

The knowledge explosion is another reason why Nebraska's isolation has been ended.

Knowledge gained through science is growing at a rapid rate every day.

The knowledge explosion means that education is more important in the lives of Nebraskans than ever before.

Things to Do

1. Guide words that will lead to new knowledge.

   STRATEGIC AIR COMMAND
   OFFUTT AIR BASE
   TELEVISION
   EDUCATIONAL TELEVISION
   SATELLITE
   INTERSTATE HIGHWAYS
   JET AIRCRAFT
   TRAVEL
   AMTRACK
   EDUCATION
   SCHOOLS

2. Hopefully, your study of changing Nebraska has given you some new understandings about your state and its people. Maybe you would like to write a statement about being a Nebraskan. Your statement can be written in any format. An essay, a poem, a song, or a picture are all statements. Think about what you want to say and how you want it said. Good luck.

I Am a Nebraskan
by
Tom Walsh

Waving rows of wheat.
Busy Omaha streets.
Red, white, black, brown, and yellow faces.
Beautiful parks and historic places.

There is more, more than my senses can record.
It is a sense of being in accord.
The crossroads of all that life is about.
Nebraska. I am a Nebraskan, I shout.

Index